Baseball
Triviology

Fun Facts from the Bleacher Seats

Neil Shalin

TRIUMPH
B O O K S

No part of this publication may be reproduced, stored in a retrieval system, or transmitted in any form by any means, electronic, mechanical, photocopying, or otherwise, without the prior written permission of the publisher, Triumph Books, 542 South Dearborn Street, Suite 750, Chicago, Illinois 60605.

Triumph Books and colophon are registered trademarks of Random House, Inc.

This book is available in quantity at special discounts for your group or organization. For further information, contact:

Triumph Books
542 South Dearborn Street
Suite 750
Chicago, Illinois 60605
(312) 939-3330
Fax (312) 663-3557
www.triumphbooks.com

Printed in U.S.A.
ISBN: 978-1-60078-540-5
Design by Patricia Frey

Contents

Introduction

Baseball history provides a great example of the old adage "the more things change, the more they stay the same." The players, the managers, the ownership, and the stadia all change over time, which makes you think about what it is you're actually rooting for when you follow your favorite team.

So what is it that inspires our allegiance to a team over a lifetime?

In realizing that the team's uniform is the one constant in baseball, comedian Jerry Seinfeld observed that we're rooting for laundry.

Longtime fans watching a game between the Yankees and the Tigers are seeing the same Yankees pinstripes against the same Tigers Old English "D" that these teams were wearing in the 1940s, and they are instantly brought back through the decades to memories of the players and games of their youth.

The Cardinals' "birds on a bat" and the word Dodgers printed in script across the team's shirt evoke memories of Stan Musial and Jackie Robinson doing battle at Ebbets Field in the good old days.

Even the uniforms themselves have undergone changes since the major leagues began in the late 1800s. From the early high-collared shirts and short-brimmed caps, to the baggy flannels with high stirrups of the twentieth century, and the double-knits of the 1970s to today's lighter fabrics, better fitting "unis," even the laundry is different. But for many teams, at least since the 1940s, the team colors, logos, lettering, and trim are pretty much the same, giving the laundry a touch of nostalgia.

This is something the young baseball followers will learn over the years: that familiarity with your team, when combined with baseball's statistics and history make the game as compelling today as it was in the days of "The Boys of Summer," "The Gas House Gang," or the last Chicago Cubs championship team in 1908. Baseball is still the National Pastime, despite what football fans claim.

Oh and there's that little gem that baseball historians believe, "baseball is the best and most unique game ever invented."

In *Baseball Triviology*, our goal is to entertain, inform, and challenge the knowledge of the young fan about the teams and players in today's game, and to introduce you to some of the old timers, in order to help you connect with the game's glorious, and sometimes less-than-glorious, past.

We hope *Baseball Triviology* will add to your interest in and knowledge of the game and give you some appreciation for its wonderful laundry.

Play ball!

Baseball
Triviology

One

The World Series

The New York Yankees took what history tells us is their rightful place atop the baseball world by defeating the defending champion Philadelphia Phillies four games to two in the 105th World Series. It was the Yankees 27th World Series win in their 40th appearance and their first since they topped the Mets 4–1 in 2000. The Yanks last met the Phillies in the Fall Classic in 1950 and swept the team known as "The Whiz Kids" 4–0.

Hideki Matsui won the Series MVP award by hitting .615, striking three homers, and knocking in eight runs in only 13 at-bats, including a record-tying six RBIs in Game 6. He became the first Japanese-born player and the first full-time designated hitter to win the series MVP Award. Matsui, who had been a Yankee for seven years, signed as a free agent with the Angels for the 2010 season.

Andy Pettitte was the winning pitcher in two games, making it five World Series victories in his career. It was also his record-setting 18th postseason career win.

Mariano Rivera had a pair of saves, increasing his career total to a record 11 World Series Saves.

1

Also coming up big for the Yankees were shortstop and captain Derek Jeter, who had 11 hits and batted .407; catcher Jorge Posada, who knocked in five runs; and outfielder Johnny Damon, who batted .364. Damon, too, was gone after the season, as he signed with the Tigers.

Quiz!

1. One member of the Phillies set the all-time record for striking out the most times in a World Series, 13. Who was it?
2. What was the name of the old-time Yankees pitcher who threw the only World Series perfect game in 1956?
3. The World Series has been played every year since 1903 but it did not take place in 1904 and 1994. In 1904 the Giants, who won the National League pennant, but refused to meet the Red Sox because of old grudges they had with the American League when it was established in 1901. Why was there no World Series in 1994?
4. Twice the World Series ended on a walk-off home run. In 1960 this was accomplished in the seventh game by a Pittsburgh Pirates second baseman who is now in the Hall of Fame, and in 1993 it was done in the sixth game by a Toronto Blue Jays outfielder. Name these two former stars.
5. Over the years, two Yankees were given their nicknames because of their heroics in the postseason. Which former Yankee was named Mr. October, and which present Yankee was dubbed Mr. November?

Answers
1. Ryan Howard
2. Don Larsen
3. Because the baseball players were on strike for the last month-and-a-half of the season and the World Series was canceled.
4. Bill Mazeroski in 1960 and Joe Carter in 1993.
5. Mr. October is Reggie Jackson, and Mr. November is Derek Jeter.

Derek Jeter leaps over Carlos Ruiz of the Philadelphia Phillies to turn a double play on a ball hit by Matt Stairs during the eighth inning of Game 5 of the World Series on Monday, November 2, 2009, in Philadelphia. *(AP Photo/David J. Phillip)*

Second baseman Chase Utley was the hitting star for the Phillies with five home runs and eight RBIs.

Cliff Lee got the decision in both of the Phils' victories. Lee also found a new home in the off-season when he was traded to the Seattle Mariners and has since been dealt again to the Texas Rangers.

World Series Memories in the Television Age

Two of the most famous walk-off home runs in history did not end the Series but they're forever ingrained in the public memory thanks to frequent exposure on highlight reels and in documentary films.

1. October 21, 1975: In the sixth game of the 1975 Series with Cincinnati leading three games to two at Fenway Park and the score tied 6–6 in the bottom of the 12th inning, Boston catcher Carlton Fisk led off with a solo shot over the monster in left field to tie the series at three games apiece. The reason the home run is so famous is that the camera stayed on Fisk after he hit the ball as he waved wildly with both hands trying to will the ball fair. (The Reds went on to win the seventh game and the championship.)

2. October 15, 1988: The underdog Los Angeles Dodgers trailed the first game of the 1988 World Series 4–3. With two out in the ninth, manager Tommy Lasorda sent a hobbling Kirk Gibson up to hit in what would be his only plate appearance in the Series. With two out and a man on base, Gibson sent the ball into the right-field stands for a two-run homer to win the game. The camera picked up on the hero painfully circling the bases with a jogging limp as TV announcer Jack Buck said a line that lives in baseball folklore: "I don't believe what I just saw."

Deacon Really Took One for the Team

Charles "Deacon" Phillippe was a pitcher for the Pittsburgh Pirates in the early part of the twentieth century. Going into the 1903 World Series, the first World Series ever, against the Boston Americans (later the Red Sox) he was a five-time 20-game winner and opened the Series against Boston ace Cy Young.

Due to illness and an injury suffered by the Pirates' other two starting pitchers, Phillippe was pressed into a heavier workload than any pitcher has ever shouldered in the World Series.

He earned the winning decision over Young in Game 1. After Boston evened the Series at 1–1, Phillippe came back two days later and won Game 3.

The Series went to Pittsburgh, and on two days rest he beat Boston a third time to give the Pirates a 3–1 lead.

The ALers came back and won Games 4 and 5 in the Series where the championship went to the first team to win five games instead of the best of seven games that was adopted in 1905 and is still the format today.

Deacon was on the mound again in Game 7, this time on three days rest. But alas, the great Pittsburgh control pitcher was running out of gas. He pitched a complete game and lost to Young 7–3. Finally, three days later, he dropped a 3–0 decision to Boston to give the American League the first World Championship.

Phillippe's line for the Series in which he tossed five complete games was three wins and two losses (that's the most decisions ever by a pitcher in a World Series) with 44 innings pitched, another record. His 19 runs and 38 hits allowed are also records, but remember, it was an eight-game series.

Deacon paid for his team spirit and courage. He was out for a portion of the following season with a sore arm but came back to register his sixth 20-win season in 1905.

An arm injury reduced his effectiveness in 1906, and he was never the same again. He finally retired in 1911.

Phillippe was one of the great control pitchers of the day, in fact, of all time. He averaged fewer walks per nine-inning game than any pitcher in history.

The actor Ryan Phillippe is a distant relative of the old-time Pirates pitcher, and to honor the old Pirates hurler, Phillippe and his then-wife, actor Reese Witherspoon, named their youngest son Deacon.

Prominent Players Who Never Appeared in a World Series
(Not included are players from the Negro Leagues, who didn't get to play in the majors before Jackie Robinson broke the color line in 1947, and players whose career ended before the first World Series in 1903.)

Catchers: Joe Torre
First basemen: Don Mattingly, Frank Thomas (on the White Sox roster in 2005 but didn't play), Andrés Galarraga, Julio Franco, George Sisler (HOF), Rafael Palmeiro, Mickey Vernon
Second basemen: Rod Carew (HOF), Ryne Sandberg (HOF), Napoleon Lajoie (HOF)
Shortstops: Ernie Banks (HOF), Luke Appling (HOF), Cecil Travis, Alan Trammell
Third basemen: Ron Santo, Dick Allen, Buddy Bell
Outfielders: Ken Griffey Jr., Ralph Kiner (HOF), Billy Williams (HOF), Andre Dawson (HOF), Harry Heilmann (HOF), Dale Murphy, Sammy Sosa, Harold Baines, Jose Cruz, Juan Gonzalez, Dave Kingman, Rocky Colavito, Bobby Bonds, Ken Williams
Designated hitter: Edgar Martinez
Pitchers: Ferguson Jenkins (HOF), Phil Niekro (HOF), Jim Bunning (HOF), Ted Lyons (HOF), Gaylord Perry (HOF), Rick Sutcliffe, Wilbur Cooper, Larry Jackson, Frank Tanana, Lindy McDaniel, Dan Plesac, Hooks Dauss, Mel Harder, Lee Smith

San Francisco's rookie starter Madison Bumgarner throws during the first inning of Game 4 of the World Series against the Texas Rangers on October 31, 2010, in Arlington, Texas. The Giants won the game 4–0 to take a 3–1 lead in the Series. *(AP Photo/Matt Campbell)*

Two

The Curse of the Bambino

"There are only two seasons—winter and baseball."

—Bill Veeck

In 2004 and 2005 the Boston Red Sox and the Chicago White Sox each won a World Series and in doing so overturned a pair of supposed baseball jinxes that had lasted nearly a century.

In 2004, a team that called themselves "The Idiots" brought to an end the Boston Red Sox's "Curse of the Bambino" that dominated the collective psyche of the team's fans for so long. The following year, the Chicago White Sox finally exorcised the ghosts of the Black Sox, who conspired with gamblers to purposely lose the 1919 World Series.

The Red Sox had not won the Grand Prize since 1918 when Babe Ruth was the ace of their pitching staff before he was converted into an outfielder to take advantage of his "gate appeal" every day. And two years later, he was traded to the Yankees in the most infamous bad trade in baseball history.

What isn't generally discussed is that in addition to The Babe, over the next few years Red Sox owner Harry Frazee also sent most of his other great pitchers to New York, including Hall of Famers Herb Pennock and Waite Hoyt as well as catcher Wally Schang and shortstop Everett Scott.

In fact, most of the Yankees pitching staff that dominated the AL—including other big names such as Carl Mays, Sad Sam Jones, and Bullet Joe Bush—were former Red Sox.

Through the years, the BoSox were hapless during the 1920s and '30s, not quite good enough with a powerful lineup led by Ted Williams in the '40s, and alternately, hapless, dull, and strong but "cursed" ever since.

However, the most frustrating seasons, the ones that most fed the myth, were:

- 1946 team that took the Cardinals to seven games in the World Series and lost.
- 1949 team when the Beantowners lost the pennant by one game to the Yankees after being one game ahead going into the final two games of the season.
- 1967 and 1975 when Boston lost two more seven-game championship series to the Cardinals and Reds, respectively.
- 1978 when the Yankees beat them in a one-game playoff on Bucky Dent's home run.
- The devastating loss to the Mets in 1986 when Boston thought it had the Series wrapped up in the late innings of Game 6, only to lose the final two games.

Those losses by Red Sox teams that *could* have and in some cases *should* have won are what jinxes are made of for people who believe in such things.

Yes, it was all because the Bambino was sent to the Yankees.

But the Idiots changed all that. The team was led by Manny Ramirez's monster season of 43 homers, 130 RBIs, and a .308 average plus the sparkling pitching of Curt Schilling and Pedro Martinez.

It was outfielder Johnny Damon, who hit .304 and scored 123 runs that season, who coined the term "The Idiots" when he was asked how the Red Sox expected to beat the Yankees.

"We're not going to try to figure it out," Damon said to a reporter during the season. "We're just a bunch of idiots. We're just going to throw the ball, hit the ball, catch the ball. We want to keep the thinking process out of it."

The Idiots got into the playoffs via the wild card, swept the Angels in the first round of the playoffs, and in the American League Championship Series, they staged the most stunning comeback in major league postseason history over the hated Yankees to earn a trip to the World Series.

The Red Sox were down three games to none, trailing 4-3 in the ninth inning of Game 4 and facing the Yankees' great closer, Mariano Rivera. Another disappointing ending seemed certain.

Rivera walked Kevin Millar. Manager Terry Francona pinch-ran for Millar with Dave Roberts, who stole second base. Bill Mueller knocked Roberts in with a single to send the game to extra innings. And David Ortiz won the game with a two-run homer in the 12th.

The Sox went on to sweep the next three games to advance to the World Series where they made short work of the Cardinals 4-0.

The ghost of the Bambino finally stopped haunting Beantown, and the Red Sox followed their World Series success with a second championship in 2007.

Quiz!

1. Name the three Boston Red Sox left fielders whose careers spanned the 1930s to the 1980s and are in the Hall of Fame.
2. This switch-hitting Red Sox catcher was the starting receiver for the 2004 championship team.
3. This right field foul pole in Fenway Park is named after this former great Red Sox infielder. Is it: a) Ted Williams b) Dom Dimaggio c) Bobby Doerr d) Johnny Pesky.
4. True or False? The two Red Sox pitchers with the most victories in 2004 were Mel Parnell and Tom Brewer.
5. Who is the Red Sox second baseman who was named the American League Rookie of the Year in 2007 and the MVP in 2008?

Answers
1. Ted Williams, Carl Yastrzemski, Jim Rice
2. Jason Varitek
3. Johnny Pesky
4. False; Curt Schilling was 21-6 and Pedro Martinez was 16-9
5. Dustin Pedroia

The Chicago White Sox's dry period started a year before their Boston counterparts when they won the 1917 American League pennant with a nine-game lead over the Red Sox and went on to win the Series 4–2 over the New York Giants. With a team led by future Hall of Famers Eddie Collins, Red Faber, and Ray Schalk and 28-game winner Ed Cicotte, and the great hitter "Shoeless" Joe Jackson, the White Sox seemed to be on their way to being longtime contenders for the title.

Dave Roberts of the Boston Red Sox hoists the World Series trophy while riding the shoulders of pitcher Mike Timlin after winning the World Series with a 3–0 win over the St. Louis Cardinals in Game 4 of the World Series in St. Louis.

After dropping to sixth place in the 1918 war-shortened season, the Pale Hose bounced back to outlast Cleveland by 3½ games the following year.

They went into the World Series against Cincinnati, the heavy favorite, but, as was revealed later, eight members of the Chicago team, including its two best pitchers and five important fielders, had arranged to throw the World Series.

While the 1920 team flirted with glory, finishing second to Cleveland by two games, at the end of the season all eight players, including "Shoeless" Joe, were banned from baseball for life.

The Black Sox stain remained with the team as it rested in the second division, for most of the next 30 years.

The White Sox team of the mid and late fifties challenged the Yankees with a team that featured pitching led by Billy Pierce and good speed and defense featuring Minnie Minoso and the Hall of Fame double-play combination of Nellie Fox at second base and Luis Aparicio at shortstop. The "Go-Go Sox" as they were known, finally made the World Series in 1959 when they lost to the Los Angeles Dodgers in six games.

With limited success over the next four decades, the White Sox were without a championship for 87 years when the 2005 team, managed by Ozzie Guillen, won it all, taking 99 games during the regular season and going 11–1 in the playoffs, including a 4–0 sweep of the Houston Astros in the Series.

Quiz!

1. Name the slugging first baseman who led the champion White Sox power attack with 40 home runs and 108 RBIs.

2. Name the right fielder who was selected as the MVP in the World Series for his clutch hitting.

3. Among the White Sox starting pitchers, he led the team in with 18 victories in 2005. Was it: a) Mark Buehrle; b) Jon Garland; c) Freddie Garcia; d) Jose Contreras.

4. White Sox great Frank Thomas, who was on the 2005 team during the season but wasn't on the roster for the World Series, goes by the nickname: a) The Auburn Flash b) The Big Smasher c)The Big Hurt d) The Chicago Tower.

5. The White Sox shortstop who made the last two great defensive plays in the ninth inning of the fourth and final game of the 2005 World Series was: a) Joe Crede b) Juan Uribe c) José Vizcaino d) Willie Harris

Three

Championship Futility

As a manager, if you don't win, you're going to be fired. If you do win, you've only put off the day you're going to be fired.

—Leo Durocher

The Red Sox and White Sox defying their frustrating histories weren't the only two historic world championships results in the first decade of this century. The 2001 Arizona Diamondbacks and 2002 California Angels (now the L.A. Angels at Anaheim) both won their first Worlds Series championships.

However, in addition to the Chicago Cubs, whose now-legendary drought goes back to 1908 (anybody can have a bad century), before winning the 2010 Series, the San Francisco Giants had to go back to their New York days and Willie Mays' catch to remember their last title in 1954. The team the Giants upset that fall, the Cleveland Indians, last sipped champagne in 1948.

And there are still eight teams who are hoping to break their seemingly endless dry-spells: the Houston Astros, Texas

Rangers, San Diego Padres, Washington Nationals, Milwaukee Brewers, Seattle Mariners, and the Colorado Rockies have never won it all.

The Chicago Cubs are the obvious standard-bearer for this list of long-time losers. After winning the World Series in both 1907 and 1908, the Cubbies, who did go to the World Series in every decade up until the 1940s have not flown the World Series championship flag since Tinker, Evers, and Chance were young men. They haven't even been to the World Series since they lost to the Tigers in seven games in 1945 at the end of World War II.

The Cleveland Indians came close in 1995. With a team loaded with future Hall of Famers and near Hall of Famers including Eddie Murray, Omar Vizquel, Jim Thome, Manny Ramirez, Albert Belle, and Orel Hershiser, the Indians fell 4–2 to the Atlanta Braves in an attempt to break the "Curse of Rocky Colavito," Cleveland's beloved home-run champion traded by general manager Frank Lane to the Tigers in 1960, when it had only been 12 years since the last Indians title.

The Tribe then went to the ninth inning of Game 7 in 1997 when they dropped the ball against the Florida Marlins, a club that grabbed its first title ever in only its fifth year of existence.

And then the Arizona Diamondbacks did the Marlins one better by topping the Yankees in 2001 in only their fourth year in the National League.

The Giants had never won in San Francisco in what they can look on as the "Curse of the Little Cable Cars That Rise Halfway to the Stars." Old Giants fans can remember their team's historic sweep of a heavily-favored Indians team in the Series with Willie

Mays' sensational catch, "The Catch" as it has come to be known, and the hitting of unsung hero Dusty Rhodes.

The Indians had won an American League record 111 games that year and boasted one of the great pitching staffs of all-time that featured four Hall of Famers: Bob Feller, Bob Lemon, Early Wynn, and Hal Newhouser. They also had a couple of barely remembered right-handers: Mike Garcia, a 19-game winner and the AL ERA champion; Art Houtteman, who won 15 games; and the lefty-righty bullpen duo of Don Mossi and Ray Narleski. Their batting order was led by Hall of Famer Larry Doby, who had two-thirds of the triple-crown with 32 home runs and 132 RBIs, batting champion Bobby Avila (.341), and powerful third baseman Al Rosen with 24 home runs, 102 RBIs, and a .300 batting average.

And the Giants beat them.

So those are the teams, the Cubs, the Indians, and the Giants (before their 2010 title), who had to delve deep into their memory banks to find their last championship season. But what about the eight teams who have never won the World Series?

The one consolation in these home cities is that these are all clubs that came into existence via expansion teams since the 1960s. The oldest of these is the Texas Rangers (formerly the Washington Senators) whose winless streak goes back to 1961, and the Houston Astros, who came into the world as the Colt 45s in 1962.

The Los Angeles Angels of Anaheim, which also joined the American League in its first expansion year of 1961, finally won it all in 2002.

The Rangers, who finally went to the World Series in 2010 before losing to the Giants in five games, and the Astros, who can take solace in the fact that they've never lost 100 games, finally made it to the fall classic in 2005. However, the White Sox were awaiting them in their Black Sox jinx-breaking year and dished out a 4-0 sweep.

In 1969, the San Diego Padres and Washington Nationals (formerly the Montreal Expos) joined the National League and the Milwaukee Brewers (now a National League team) entered the American League. None of the three have ever won the top prize.

The 1968 expansion team, the Kansas City Royals, bested the Cardinals 4-3 in the 1985 all-Missouri World Series.

The Padres made it to the World Series in 1984 but they were overpowered in five games by the American League champion Detroit Tigers.

The Seattle Mariners, an American League franchise since 1977, are still looking for their first title. In fact, the team is still looking for its first World Series appearance.

The 2001 Mariners have the distinction of sharing the lead with the 1906 Chicago Cubs by winning the most games, 116, in a regular season. The Mariners won the American League West by 14 games in 2001, and they went on to defeat Cleveland in the ALDS. But the Mariners fell to the Yankees in five games in the ALCS.

More recent additions such as the Colorado Rockies and the Tampa Bay Rays are still looking for their first title, as well.

Quiz!

1. Name at least two members of the "Killer Bees," who formed the heart of the Houston Astros lineup on some very good teams in the late 1990s and early 2000s.

2. We all know the Yankees have played in the most World Series, 40, but which team is second in most Fall Classic appearances?

3. The Yankees are also the runaway leader in World Championships with 27 and the Dodgers have only 6. Which three teams have taken home the big prize more times than the Dodgers?

4. Though they've never won a World Series, the Astros, Mariners, Expos/Nationals, and Padres have had some great runs at times during their histories. For which of these teams did each of the following trio of current or future Hall of Famers play?
   a) Ken Griffey Jr., Alex Rodriguez, Ichiro Suzuki
   b) Tony Gwynn, Dave Winfield, Trevor Hoffman
   c) Nolan Ryan, Craig Biggio, Jeff Bagwell
   d) Gary Carter, Andre Dawson, Tim Raines

5. Name the Seattle Mariners rookie who won the AL batting championship in 2001. And name the team's ace who won 20 games.

Answers

1. You would be right if you said Craig Biggio, Lance Berkman, Jeff Bagwell, Derek Bell, Sean Berry, and Tim Bogar, though you probably wouldn't say the last three.
2. The Brooklyn/Los Angeles Dodgers with 18.
3. The St. Louis Cardinals with 10, the Philadelphia/Oakland A's with nine, and the Boston Red Sox with 7.
4. a) Mariners, b) Padres, c) Astros, d) Expos
5. Ichiro Suzuki, Jamie Moyer

Four

The Core Four

Derek Jeter, Jorge Posada, and Mariano Rivera of the Yankees have been teammates longer than any trio in the history of the four major team sports, MLB, NFL, NBA, and NHL.

The three, who have led the Yankees to five world championships, most recently in 2009, and 14 postseason playoffs, joined the Bronx Bombers in 1995, so they've been playing together in the majors for 16 seasons.

That's one year longer than baseball's former all-time trio of teammates, Jim Gantner, Paul Molitor, and Robin Yount, who were together on the Brewers from 1978–92.

The second-longest Yankees record for three teammates is a tie between the group of Bill Dickey, Lefty Gomez, and Red Ruffing from 1930–42 and Whitey Ford, Elston Howard, and Mickey Mantle from 1955–67.

The 16 years that Jeter, Rivera, and Posada have spent as Yankees teammates is three seasons more than two other Yankee trios.

A fourth pinstriper, pitcher Andy Pettitte, also became a Yankee in 1995, but he left for three years (2004–06) after signing a free agent contract with the Houston Astros before returning to his original team.

Together, the quartet of Jeter, Posada, Rivera, and Pettitte is known as the "Core Four," and they've come to symbolize the stability and excellence of the latest phase of the ongoing Yankees dynasty that spans the past 90 years since the arrival of Babe Ruth in 1920 in a trade with the Boston Red Sox.

"I've been blessed because I have four guys, we played for 15 years together," Rivera told the Associated Press after last year's World Series. "And we have accomplished everything together."

"The funny thing about these guys is the team in the 1990s couldn't have won without them, and the team now couldn't have won without them," said Yankees broadcaster Paul O'Neill, who co-starred on the Core Four's first four title-winning teams. "I don't think you'll ever see that again, four constants like that."

Shortstop Jeter, the Yankees' captain for the past eight seasons, and Rivera, who is regarded by many to be the best closer of all time, are pretty much shoo-ins for early election to the Hall of Fame five years after they retire.

Posada, whose career stats are approaching those of many backstops in the Hall of Fame, has a good chance to take his place in Cooperstown, while Pettitte, with 240 career victories as of August 1, 2010, has an outside shot based on his contribution to championship teams and his postseason excellence.

While Pettitte missed two of the Yankees' 14 years in which they made it to the postseason (he made it to the playoffs once as an Astro), Jeter, Rivera, and Posada have been there for the entire ride.

Jeter summed up the feelings of the Core Four and his other Yankees teammates on the winning teams of the past 15 years

Jorge Posada, right, and Yankees closer Mariano Rivera have been teammates since 1995.
(AP Photo/Kathy Willens)

when he said, "We just want to win. That's the bottom line. I think a lot of times people may become content with one championship or a little bit of success, but we don't really reflect on what we've done in the past. We focus on the present."

Quiz!

1. Who is the only player in baseball history to win the All-Star Game and World Series MVP awards in the same year?
   a) Derek Jeter b) Andy Pettitte c) Jorge Posada d) Mariano Rivera
2. This member of the Core Four passed the great Lou Gehrig as the all-time Yankees career leader in hits.
3. In late August current Yankees third baseman Alex Rodriguez and Jorge Posada were tied for seventh on the Yankees career home-run list. Name the six people ahead of them. (Clues: Five of them are in the Hall of Fame and the sixth was a teammate of the Core Four on the championship teams between 1996 and 2000.)
4. Andy Pettitte is second to this Hall of Fame pitcher on the Yankees all-time strikeout list. Who has struck out more batters than anyone else in franchise history?
5. One member of the Core Four played sparingly for the Yankees during the 1996 season, and he was not on the team's World Series roster. Who was it?

By The Way

Mariano Rivera has saved more wins (68) for Andy Pettitte than any other reliever has saved for a particular starter in the history of baseball. In 2009, the Yankees hurlers passed the A's Bob Welch and Dennis Eckersley. In the 1980s and '90s Hall of Famer Eckersley saved 57 games for Welch.

Posada joins Yankees greats Yogi Berra and Bill Dickey as the only three catchers in franchise history with more than 1,000 career RBIs.

In addition to being the all-time Yankees leader in hits, Jeter also ranks first in team history in at-bats, second to Rickey Henderson in stolen bases 326 to 319, and second to Lou Gehrig in doubles 534 to 462.

Pettitte is second to Whitey Ford in games started as a Yankees pitcher 438 to 393, and with 203 wins, he's behind club leaders Ford (236) and Red Ruffing (231).

Rivera, of course, is way ahead of No. 2 Yankees reliever Dave Righetti 522 to 224, and he has appeared in 964 games to Righetti's 522.

Five

Albert Pujols

If Albert Pujols retired today, he would be elected to the Hall of Fame on the first ballot. That's how spectacular the Cardinals first baseman has been in the first decade of his career. Going into the 2010 season, he has earned three MVPs and has a .332 lifetime batting average.

He has led the National League:
- three times in RBIs
- three times in slugging percentage
- four times in total bases
- five times in runs scored
- once in home runs

He's been among the leaders in most hitting categories in the years he didn't lead the league. And that's not counting 2010 in which he entered September leading or near the top of the league in most hitting categories.

Pujols even has a Gold Glove.

In August, when Pujols became the third youngest man to hit 400 home runs in major league history, it called attention to his consistently superior play for the past 10 seasons.

If that weren't enough, he's also considered a great teammate, is liked and respected by both opponents and commentators, and he's been an active force for good in the community.

He's an ideal ballplayer who's already being mentioned with the best of all time, including first basemen Lou Gehrig, Jimmie Foxx, and St. Louis icon Stan Musial. "I don't know how anybody could ever be better than he is. Ever," teammate Adam Wainwright said.

And here's a sampling of what Cardinals manager Tony La Russa thinks of Pujols:

"Albert is the whole package. He commits to defense just like he does offense. He has natural talent. He's very smart and very tough-minded. He's so strong between the ears that nothing fazes him. He's a really great player. We're lucky to watch him."

Cardinals hitting coach Mitchell Page said Pujols has the best work habits he's ever seen.

And The Man himself, Stan Musial, calls Pujols the best right-handed hitter in the game.

Pujols believes that his best asset is his intelligence. "If you tell me something—I get it quickly," he said. "That's the best thing I have going for me, my ability to listen to a coach and fix what I'm doing wrong."

He also sees himself above all as a teammate who's dedicated to winning.

Since Pujols joined the team, the Cardinals have been to the postseason six times and won it all in 2006. And it's wonderful to consider that we could have another decade or more to watch Pujols play and mount his assault on the career batting records.

Let's suspend for a moment the Hall of Fame voting rule that says a player has to wait five years beyond his retirement to be voted in and give Pujols instant election to Cooperstown.

Here's a list of active players who should be in the Pujols 2010 class even if they never play another game:

First baseman: Jim Thome; shortstops: Derek Jeter, Omar Vizquel; third basemen: Alex Rodriguez, Chipper Jones; catcher: Ivan Rodriguez; outfielders: Ichiro Suzuki, Manny Ramirez, Vladimir Guerrero; pitchers: Pedro Martinez, Mariano Rivera, Trevor Hoffman.

And these recently retired players not yet on the ballot should also be enshrined. First basemen: Frank Thomas, Jeff Bagwell; second baseman: Craig Biggio; catcher: Mike Piazza; outfielders: Ken Griffey Jr.; Barry Bonds, Sammy Sosa; pitchers: Randy Johnson, Tom Glavine, Greg Maddux, Roger Clemens, John Smoltz, Curt Schilling.

And finally, let's have one big election to make the Hall of Fame complete by admitting all the deserving players in modern baseball history, including some Negro Leaguers the Veterans Committee missed.

Because the Hall of Fame is a museum, we think it would be historically incomplete to leave out anyone who should have a plaque in Cooperstown. The gambling problems of Shoeless Joe Jackson and Pete Rose can be noted on their plaques, while the steroids and performance-enhancing supplement questions can be worked out by the "Lords of Baseball," the guys who condoned and profited from the cheating in the first place.

St. Louis Cardinals first baseman Albert Pujols at-bat on Tuesday, May 25, 2010, in San Diego.
(AP Photo/Lenny Ignelzi)

So here it is—in addition to those already enshrined and the instant selections of active and recently retired players—the complete Hall of Fame of players who played after 1900. We can all argue about the selections and that's half the fun of being a sports fan and someone who has a passion for baseball and its history.

First basemen: Steve Garvey, Don Mattingly, Gil Hodges, Keith Hernandez, Buck O'Neil (Negro Leagues), Mark McGwire

Second basemen: Roberto Alomar, Pete Rose, Bingo DeMoss (Negro Leagues), Newt Allen (Negro Leagues), Buddy Myer, Sammy T. Hughes (Negro Leagues), Larry Doyle

Shortstops: Barry Larkin, Dick Lundy (Negro Leagues), Cecil Travis, John Beckwith (Negro Leagues), Maury Wills, Marty Marion, Alan Trammell, Dave Concepcion

Third basemen: Ron Santo, Dick Allen, Ken Boyer, Oliver Marcelle (Negro Leagues), Stan Hack

Outfielders: Tony Oliva, Curt Flood, Minnie Minoso, Vada Pinson, Dave Parker, Sherry McGee, Bill Wright (Negro Leagues), Spot Poles (Negro Leagues), Dom Dimaggio, Shoeless Joe Jackson, Roger Maris, Gavvy Cravath, Ken Williams, Dale Murphy, Jose Canseco, Juan Gonzalez, Albert Belle

Catchers: Elston Howard, Thurman Munson, Joe Torre, Ted Simmons, Bill Freehan,

Pitchers: Jim Kaat, Bert Blyleven, Jack Morris, Tommy John, Dick Redding (Negro Leagues), Bill Byrd (Negro Leagues), Luis Tiant, Don Newcombe, Billy Pierce, Carl Mays, Allie Reynolds, Urban Shocker, Lee Smith, Chet Brewer (Negro Leagues), Bucky Walters

Designated Hitter: Edgar Martinez

Executive Director of the Major League Baseball Players Association: Marvin Miller

Pitching coach: Johnny Sain

Six

The Cy Young Award

The retirement of Randy Johnson in 2010 brought up memories of the great Cy Young, who last pitched in the majors about a century ago.

Not only because Johnson was a five-time winner of the Cy Young Award as the best pitcher in his league, but also because the Big Unit leaves the game as a 300-game winner, and there's speculation that he could be the last of the breed.

When you consider how much the game has changed and how those changes have made it more difficult to accumulate career wins in large numbers. It seems unlikely that any pitcher will reach the 300 mark in the foreseeable future.

The active career leader is Jamie Moyer with 267 and he's 45 years old, so it would be a surprise if he can stick around and pitch effectively enough to put up 33 more wins on the board.

Next in line is Andy Pettitte with 240, and he's already talking about retiring, while third is Pedro Martinez at 219, but he could be just about at the end of the line.

There are two main reasons for the more modest career victory numbers.

First, in recent decades baseball has gone to the five-man starting rotation, removing a significant number of starts per season for what used to be a starting four.

Also the frequent use of relief pitchers—middle-inning relievers, set-up men, and then closers—has made the complete game a rare statistic for even the best of pitchers. Starting pitchers are usually on strict pitch counts to make sure they don't risk injury.

Cy Young's record of 511 wins, which will certainly never be broken, and his 316 losses, which is also safe, included 749 complete games out of 815 starts.

To give you an idea of the enormity of the task for modern and future pitchers would need to perform to equal Young, remember that if a pitcher wins 20 games for 20 straight years, he's still only at 400, which is far short of the record.

Johnson, by comparison, who is surely headed for the Hall of Fame with a lifetime record of 303–166, started 618 games and completed 100.

Young had 40 or more starts 11 times in his career. He had 15 20-victory seasons, 12 of them with 25 or more and five seasons with more than 30 wins.

While it is possible for the modern era to produce a 300-game winner, other factors are required such as staying relatively injury free, pitching for a contender that can give him the run support he needs, and maintaining the consistency to put him in a position to reach the milestone.

Saying that it can't be done can certainly throw up a challenge for contemporary aces such as Johan Santana, Roy Halladay, and CC Sabathia, and if all the pieces fall into place, it is possible.

Arizona Diamondbacks pitcher Randy Johnson delivers a pitch during the fourth inning of a baseball game against the San Francisco Giants on Thursday, May 29, 2008, in Phoenix. Johnson struck out the Giants' Dan Ortmeier in the seventh inning for his 4,672nd career strikeout, tying him for second place all-time with Roger Clemens. *(AP Photo/Dave Sharpe)*

The first winner of the Cy Young Award as the outstanding pitcher in baseball was Don Newcombe of the Brooklyn Dodgers in 1956. That year Newcombe had one of the truly outstanding pitching seasons of all time with a 27–7 season.

There were 10 more Cy Young Awards given for the best pitcher in the major leagues before it was decided in 1967 to award one prize for each league.

Here's the chance to test your knowledge about the game's best pitchers since 1956.

Quiz!

1. Identify the right hander who started with the Boston Red Sox and later pitched for the Blue Jays, Yankees, and Astros before retiring after the 2007 season with the most Cy Young Awards—seven to his credit. (Clue: He won at least one of his Cy Young Awards for each of those teams.)
2. The American League Cy Young Award winner in 2009 was a member of the Kansas City Royals. Who is he?
3. The National League had a repeat winner. Who is this National League Western Division pitcher who won his second Cy Young Award in a row in 2009?
4. Randy Johnson is second on the list with five Cy Young Awards. He won the AL award in 1995 while pitching for the Seattle Mariners. His other four came in four successive years (1999–2002) while he pitched for this National League team. Name the team.
5. Tied for third on the list of most Cy Young Award winners are Steve Carlton, a lefty Hall of Famer who won them in the 1970s and '80s as a member of the Phillies, and a National League pitcher who also won four in a row. This

right-hander, who retired in 2008, won his first award when he played for the Chicago Cubs in 1992 and his next three when he was the ace of the Atlanta Braves staff in 1993, '94 and '95. (Again to compare a modern-day pitcher to Cy Young, this pitcher's only career 20-victory seasons were in 1992 and '93, and he retired with 355 career victories.)

6. The National League Cy Young award winner in both 1968 and 1970 had been a basketball star at Creighton University and later played for the Harlem Globetrotters. Who is he?

7. Name the National League Cy Young winner in 1979. He was a relief pitcher with the Chicago Cubs who saved 37 games that year. He's also in the Hall of Fame.

8. Name the American League Cy Young winner in 1992. He was also a reliever with the Oakland A's who saved 51 games that year. He's also in the Hall of Fame.

9. Since the Atlanta Braves pitcher in Question 5 won his three straight Cy Young Awards in 1993, '94 and '95, two of his Atlanta teammates won the prize in two of the next three years. Who were these two pitchers who were still active in 2009?

10. Name the Dodgers left-hander who won three Cy Young Awards in the 1960s and then retired due to arthritis trouble at the age of 30 after winning his third.

Answers
1. Roger Clemens
2. Zack Greinke
3. Tim Lincecum
4. Arizona Diamondbacks
5. Greg Maddux
6. Bob Gibson
7. Bruce Sutter
8. Dennis Eckersley
9. John Smoltz (1996), Tom Glavine (1998)
10. Sandy Koufax.

Hall of Fame pitcher Sandy Koufax was the first three-time Cy Young Award winner in Major League Baseball history. The southpaw spent his entire career (1955–66) with the Brooklyn/Los Angeles Dodgers. *(AP Photo)*

More about Sandy Koufax

- Koufax's three Cy Young Awards, 1963, '65, and '66 were all by unanimous vote.
- In 1963 he also won the National League MVP Award.
- In all three of his Cy Young Award–winning years, he won the triple crown of pitching as he led the NL in wins, strikeouts, and earned run average.
- He was the first pitcher in baseball history to throw four no-hitters, including a perfect game.

Seven

The Rookies

If even half the praise the experts are showering on this year's rookie class is accurate, there's a whole new era dawning in Major League Baseball.

While they're quick to make comparisons to other years that included rookies who went on to All-Star and Hall of Fame careers, some observers claim that based on first-year performances by a class led by pitchers Stephen Strasburg and Mike Leake, catcher Buster Posey, and outfielder Jason Heyward, this could rank with the best groups of all time.

Top 10 Rookies of 2010

Here are some, but by no means all, of those debutants who baseball fans should be talking about for years to come:

1. **Stephen Strasburg, RHP, Washington Nationals, 22 years old.**
   The most heralded pitcher to come to the majors in a generation, Strasburg hasn't disappointed. Through early August 2010, his stats were impressive: 5-2, 75 Ks, 2.32 ERA, 1.07 WHIP. His spectacular debut showed that he could be one of the pitching greats. In late August, he underwent Tommy John surgery, and he will be out for 12–18 months.

Washington Nationals pitcher Stephen Strasburg delivers to the Arizona Diamondbacks during the fourth inning of a baseball game in Washington D.C. on Sunday, August 15, 2010. The Nationals defeated the Diamondbacks 5–3. *(AP Photo/Ann Heisenfelt)*

2. **Jason Heyward, OF, Atlanta Braves, 21 years old.** In his first 81 games, the "Jay-Hey Kid" posted a .270 batting average, 11 HR, and 50 RBI. He was selected for the 2010 All-Star Game, and he was named April and May National League Rookie of the Month. He's the whole package, a five-tool player who knows the game and is mature way beyond his years.

3. **Buster Posey, C, San Francisco Giants, 23 years old.** Through early August his stats were impressive: .350 batting average, 8 HR, 34 RBIs. Posey is a powerful, disciplined hitter, and he's developing into a good big-league catcher who can handle the pitching staff. He starred in the postseason as the Giants marched to their first World Series championship since 1954.

4. **Brennan Boesch, OF, Detroit Tigers, 25 years old.** He was the big rookie surprise of the season before going down for the year with an injury. This power-hitter took the AL Rookie of the Month Award in both May and June and was chosen for the All-Star Game.

5. **Austin Jackson, OF, Detroit Tigers, 23 years old.** This fleet-footed flychaser came to the Tigers from the Yankees in the Curtis Granderson trade and proceeded to earn the April AL Rookie of the Month award. Jackson was hitting above .300 late in the season, and he showed he can beat you in the field and on the base paths.

6. **Starlin Castro, SS, Chicago Cubs, 20 years old.** He still has some maturing to do in the field, but Castro has proved he can hit major league pitching by staying around the .300 mark all year.

7. **Mike Leake, RHP, Cincinnati Reds, 22 years old.** Leake isn't the most overpowering pitcher around, but he's got a variety of pitches, good command, and he's a battler. He's another rookie who has been a bit of a surprise. He spent a lot of time on the disabled list late in the season.

8. **Ike Davis, 1B, New York Mets, 23 years old.** Davis started off on a hot streak, but he still needs more patience at the plate in order to grow into his potential as one of the game's great sluggers. He's a terrific fielder and has a strong arm.
9. **Neftali Feliz, RP, Texas Rangers, 22 years old.** This flame-throwing reliever entered the season as the Rangers top prospect, took over the closer role early on, and established himself as one of the best in the game. He finished the season with 40 saves, a record for a rookie.
10. **Mike Stanton, OF, Florida Marlins, 20 years old.** Stanton is a great athlete with awesome power who can run and is a natural right fielder. He's a future superstar who has been compared to Hall of Famer Dave Winfield.

Other Top Rookies of 2010
Catcher: Carlos Santana (Indians), John Jaso (Rays)
First base: Gaby Sanchez (Marlins), Justin Smoak (Mariners)
Second base: Reid Brignac (Rays), Neil Walker (Pirates), Scott Sizemore (Tigers)
Shortstop: Ian Desmond (Nationals), Alcides Escobar (Brewers)
Third base: Danny Valencia (Twins)
Outfield: Domonic Brown (Phillies), Tyler Colvin (Cubs)
Pitchers: Jamie Garcia (Cardinals), Mitch Talbot (Indians), Brian Matusz (Orioles), Madison Bumgarner (Giants), Jhoulys Chacin (Rockies), Jonny Venters (Braves), Jeremy Hellickson (Rays)

Young Guns
While they're not members of the 2010 rookie class, there are many established major leaguers who are 26 years old and younger who should be stars for a number of years. Let's see if you can identify the young veterans we describe in these questions:

Quiz!

1. This Yankees All-Star right-hander started the 2010 season with a 12–4 record and pitched in his first All-Star Game.
2. This crafty Giants right-hander won the National League Cy Young Award in 2008 and 2009.
3. This Oakland A's reliever enjoyed a fine sophomore season after winning the American League Rookie of the Year Award in 2009.
4. The runner-up for the 2009 Rookie of the Year Award was this Texas Rangers shortstop.
5. By now a Chicago White Sox pitching mainstay, this right-hander has posted double-digit victories the past three years.
6. An outfielder for the Marlins, he was the 2009 National Rookie of the Year.
7. This tall Atlanta Braves pitcher won 11 games as a rookie in 2009 and is now a key member of the team's rotation.
8. The winner of both the Gold Glove and the Silver Slugger Awards in 2009, this Washington third baseman hit well over 100 home runs before his 26th birthday.
9. Identify the 23-year-old right fielder who was voted the Arizona Diamondbacks MVP in 2009.
10. Name the left-handed pitcher who was the first pick in the 2007 Amateur Draft who is now the ace of the Rays pitching staff.
11. This Rockies right-hander got off to a 17–3 record in 2010.
12. Identify the 24-year-old Mariners ace who in 2010 had already been in the majors for six years.
13. This Rays All-Star third baseman is expected to be an all-time great at the hot corner.
14. This Dodgers outfielder is equally dangerous with the bat, on the base paths, and in the field.
15. This Venezuelan outfielder had a breakout year for the Rockies in 2010.

The Rookie of the Year Award

The first time the Rookie of the Year Award was given in 1947 it was awarded to one person for all of baseball rather than to one player in each league. The recipient in that historic first year was the Brooklyn Dodgers' Jackie Robinson. He earned the award with a .297 batting average and 125 runs scored while leading the Dodgers to the National League pennant.

To honor his memory, the award was named "The Jackie Robinson Rookie of the Year Award" in 1987 on the 40th anniversary of Robinson breaking the color barrier.

In 1948, the Braves went to the World Series and their rookie shortstop, Alvin Dark, who would later star for the New York Giants and captain them to a pair of World Series appearances, won the award with a .322 average.

The first year the award was split into one honoree for each league was 1949. Robinson's teammate, Don Newcombe, who went 17–8 with five shutouts, won for the National League, while Roy Sievers, who went on to a long career as an American League slugger, won it for the junior circuit.

Those first four recipients stayed in the majors for many years and continued to shower themselves in glory, with Robinson the only one of those pioneer Rookie of the Year Award recipients to make it to the Hall of Fame.

Over the years, many great ballplayers have won the award, but winning Rookie of the Year hasn't necessarily been a predictor of long-term greatness. Many who made a big splash in their first year faded quickly because of injury or because their skills didn't continue to develop. You probably haven't heard the names Harry Byrd (AL '52), Earl Williams (NL '71), Butch Metzger (NL co-MVP '76), or Joe Charboneau (AL '80) lately.

Which league do you think would win a mythical game pitting the All-Time Rookie of the Year rosters against each other? Although we're leaving out some pretty fine ballplayers, these players could make up a formidable team of rookie award winners for each league. You make the choice.

American League
First Base: Eddie Murray, Orioles ('75, Hall of Fame); Mark McGwire, A's ('87)

Second Base: Rod Carew, Twins ('67, Hall of Fame); Lou Whitaker, Tigers ('77)

Shortstop: Derek Jeter, Yankees ('96); Luis Aparicio, White Sox ('56, Hall of Fame); Ozzie Guillen, White Sox ('85)

Third Base: In a position switch from shortstop Cal Ripken Jr., Orioles ('82, Hall of Fame); Evan Longoria, Rays ('08); Nomar Garciaparra, Red Sox ('97)

Outfield: Tony Oliva, Twins ('64); Fred Lynn, Red Sox ('75); Jose Canseco, A's ('86); Tim Salmon, Angels ('93); Carlos Beltran, Royals ('99); Ichiro Suzuki, Mariners ('01,)

Catcher: Carlton Fisk, Red Sox ('72, Hall of Fame); Thurman Munson, Yankees ('70); Sandy Alomar Jr., Indians ('90)

Pitchers: Herb Score, Indians ('55); Gary Peters, White Sox ('63); Stan Bahnsen, Yankees ('68); Dave Righetti, Yankees ('81); Gregg Olson, Orioles ('89); Kazuhiro Sasaki, Mariners (OO); Huston Street, A's ('05); Justin Verlander, Tigers ('06); Andrew Bailey, A's ('09)

National League
First base: Orlando Cepeda, Giants ('58, Hall of Fame); Willie McCovey, Giants ('59, Hall of Fame); Jeff Bagwell, Astros ('91); Albert Pujols, Cardinals ('01)

Second base: Jackie Robinson, Dodgers ('47, Hall of Fame); Jim Gilliam, Dodgers ('53); Pete Rose, Reds ('63)

Shortstop: Alvin Dark, Braves ('48); Hanley Ramirez, Marlins ('06)

Never Played in the Minor Leagues

First base: Ernie Banks
Second base: Frankie Frisch
Shortstop: Dick Groat, Jack Barry
Third base: Eddie Yost
Outfield: Al Kaline, Ethan Allen, Mel Ott
Pitchers: Sandy Koufax, Carl Scheib, Milt Gaston, Johnny Antonelli, Eddie Plank, Jack Coombs, Danny MacFayden, Catfish Hunter, Bob Feller, Billy O'Dell, Eppa Rixey, Tom Zachary, Ted Lyons

One of our infielders or pitchers will have to be converted to a catcher. Otherwise, we're solid all the way around with 10 Hall of Famers.

(Note: Dick Groat was a two-time college All-American basketball player at Duke, and in 1952 he was named the Helms Foundation College Basketball Player of the Year. He played one year for the then Fort Wayne Pistons and averaged in double figures before going into the army. When he was discharged he decided to concentrate on baseball with the Pittsburgh Pirates.)

Third Base: Dick Allen, Phillies ('64); Scott Rolen, Phillies ('97)

Outfield: Willie Mays, Giants ('51, Hall of Fame); Bill Virdon, Cardinals ('55); Frank Robinson, Reds ('56, Hall of Fame); Frank Howard, Dodgers ('60); Billy Williams, Cubs ('61, Hall of Fame); Gary Matthews, Giants ('73); Andre Dawson, Cubs ('77, Hall of Fame); Darryl Strawberry, Mets ('83); Ryan Braun, Brewers ('07)

Catchers: Johnny Bench, Reds ('68, Hall of Fame); Mike Piazza, Dodgers ('93); Benito Santiago, Padres ('87)

Pitchers: Don Newcombe, Dodgers ('49); Jack Sanford, Phillies ('57); Tom Seaver, Mets ('68, Hall of Fame); Jon Matlack, Mets ('72); Rick Sutcliffe, Dodgers ('79); Fernando Valenzuela, Dodgers ('81); Dwight Gooden, Mets ('84); Todd Worrell, Cardinals ('86); Hideo Nomo, Dodgers ('95); Kerry Wood, Cubs ('95)

Eight

Hitting for the Cycle

On July 16, 2010, catcher Bengie Molina of the Texas Rangers, hit for the cycle in an 8–4 win over the Red Sox—that is, he had a single, double, triple, and home run in the same game. Hitting for the cycle is a relatively rare occurrence in Major League Baseball, it's been done only 291 times since 1880.

It is surprising that Bengie Molina, long regarded as one of the best defensive catchers in baseball, would be one of four players to have done so in 2010.

Molina's achievement is even more interesting because the cycle includes hitting a triple, and the Rangers catcher is known as being one of the slowest runners in the league. In fact, he has hit only five triples in his 12-year major league career. Also, Molina's home run, his third hit of the day, was a Grand Slam, and he became only the ninth cycle-hitter in baseball history to include a bases-loaded homer in his cycle.

After starting with a single and double in his first two at-bats, Molina, whom the Rangers had acquired just two weeks before, added the grand slam in the fifth inning. However, even though he

Bengie Molina, catcher for the Texas Rangers (right) beats the throw on a stand-up triple as Boston Red Sox third baseman Adrian Beltre fields the throw during the eighth inning of a baseball game in Boston on Friday, July 16, 2010. Molina hit for the cycle in the game.
(AP Photo/Charles Krupa)

was aware that he could get the cycle, he wasn't thinking triple when he came up for his fourth turn at the plate.

"When he [Red Sox center fielder Eric Patterson] dropped the ball, that's when you're thinking, 'got to go, got to go,'" Molina said. Molina, who was 4-for-4 with four RBIs for the day, was replaced by pinch-runner Joaquin Arias, who later scored.

Molina became the 15th catcher in major league history to hit for the cycle, a list that includes three Hall of Famers, Ray Schalk (1922), Mickey Cochrane (in both 1932 and 1933), and Carlton Fisk (1984), but he was the first catcher to include a grand slam in his big day.

The feat was the fifth cycle in Rangers history; the most recent was by Ian Kinsler in 2009.

The night that Molina hit for the cycle, his younger brother Yadier homered for the Cardinals.

Since Molina's cycle, two other major leaguers have also accomplished the feat. One week later, Kelly Johnson did it on July 23, and then on the 31st of that month, Carlos Gonzalez of the Colorado Rockies came through. That makes four for this season with Jody Gerut of the Milwaukee Brewers doing the trick on May 8. There were eight hit last year, and it has been done 50 times since the year 2000.

The natural cycle, which means the player hit a single, double, triple and home run in order, has been done only 14 times in history, the last one by Brad Wilkerson of the Montreal Expos in 2003.

There have been three reverse natural cycles (home run, triple, double, single) which were hit by Jim Fregosi in 1968, Luke Scott in 2006, and Carlos Gomez in 2008.

The record for most career cycles is three, and it's a three-way tie among John Reilly, who played in the late nineteenth century, plus a pair of sluggers from the 1920s and '30s—the Yankees' Bob

Meusel, who did it twice in 1926 and then again in 1928; and Babe Herman, who did it twice in 1931 for the Dodgers and then his third came in 1933 when he was a member of the Cubs.

Honus Wagner, Ty Cobb, and Babe Ruth never hit for the cycle, nor did Ted Williams, Willie Mays, or Hank Aaron. And Albert Pujols hasn't done it as of the 2010 season.

Yankees Hall of Fame second baseman Tony Lazzeri is the only man in baseball history to have hit for the natural cycle and do it with a grand slam when he accomplished it in 1932, coincidentally in the same game in which Lou Gehrig hit four home runs.

Bob Meusel and Babe Herman

Bob Meusel and Babe Herman, the two modern players who hit for the cycle three times each in their careers, are two of the better-hitting outfielders in the era between the World Wars who have not been, and probably never will be, elected to the Hall of Fame.

Meusel batted fifth behind Babe Ruth and Lou Gehrig in the Yankees' lineup known as Murderers' Row. He had a lifetime .309 batting average, drove in 100 runs or more five times, and led the American League in home runs and RBIs in 1925. He played for six Yankees World Series teams and three World Series champions.

It was generally agreed that Meusel had the best outfield arm in the majors. He led the league in outfield assists several times early in his career, but after that runners were reluctant to test his arm. It was said that the great Ty Cobb wouldn't run on Meusel.

He was usually the Yankees left fielder, but he took over in right in the cities where right field was the sun field. Meusel often switched positions because the Babe didn't like to look into the sun.

Herman, a great hitter, but a notoriously poor fielder and base-runner, hit for a .324 average in a career that spanned the 1920s and '30s. Known for his frequent fielding and base-running errors, both physical and mental, Herman was the batter in one of the most famous goof-ups in baseball.

As legend has it, he tripled into a triple play, which is actually an exaggeration. He did, however, double into a double play.

It took place during his rookie year of 1926 when Herman was a member of the Brooklyn Dodgers' hapless "Daffiness Boys," who

Quiz!

1. We mentioned that Bengie Molina's brother, Yadier, is a catcher for the Cardinals. There is another Molina brother who is also a major league catcher. Please give us his name and his team.
2. Bengie Molina hit for the cycle as a member of the Texas Rangers, a team that acquired him two weeks before his accomplishment. On what team did Molina begin the 2010 season?
3. What is Bengie Molina's nickname?
4. What American League award did Molina win in both 2002 and 2003 as a member of the California Angels?
5. Eight players hit for the cycle in 2009, which is tied with 1933 for the most ever in a season. Ian Kinsler was one player who did it. How many of the other seven can you name?

Answers
1. Jose Molina of the Toronto Blue Jays
2. The San Francisco Giants
3. Big Money
4. The Gold Glove Award as the best defensive catcher in the league.
5. Orlando Hudson (Dodgers), Jason Kubel, Michael Cuddyer (Twins), Melky Cabrera (Yankees), Troy Tulowitzki (Rockies), Felix Pie (Orioles), B.J. Upton (Rays)

Felix Pie of the Baltimore Orioles smiles after getting hit in the face with a shaving cream pie after the team defeated the Los Angeles Angels 16–6 on August 14, 2009, in Baltimore. Pie hit for the cycle during the game. *(AP Photo/Rob Carr)*

got that nickname because their games often turned out to be an adventure, and not in a good way.

With the bases loaded and nobody out, Herman doubled to right and tried to stretch it into a triple. And was he surprised to find two of his teammates already on third base! Pitcher Dazzy Vance had advanced from second and was held up because he was a slow runner, and Chick Fewster, who had legged it there from first, had stopped because he was afraid he'd be called out if he passed Vance. The third baseman tagged all three, but the ump called Vance safe because he had gotten there first. Fewster and Herman were both called out. Hank DeBerry, who was on third when the play started, scored what turned out to be the winning run.

Nine

The All-Star Game

The National League's 3–1 win in the 2010 All-Star Game in Anaheim snapped a 12-game American League winning streak (although there was that one tie in 2002).

The victory gave the National League a 41–38–2 edge in the midsummer classic since it started in 1933 and brought back memories of when the senior circuit dominated the All-Star competition. In fact, between 1960 and 1982, the National League totally dominated with a 23–2–1 advantage. In the years 1959 to 1962, two All-Star Games were played.

Early in the competition, it was the American League, led by such sluggers as Babe Ruth, Lou Gehrig, Jimmie Foxx, Hank Greenberg, Ted Williams, and Joe DiMaggio, that won 12 of the first 16 games between 1933 and 1949.

The first All-Star Game was played at Comiskey Park in Chicago in 1933 and was won by the American League 4–2. It was the brainchild of *Chicago Tribune* sports editor Arch Ward, and it was intended to be only a one-time event, but it quickly became a tradition and the Midsummer Classic that it is today.

In 1934, the game moved to the Polo Grounds in New York. The American League won again, but that game is now most famous for the legendary pitching performance by Carl Hubbell of the hometown Giants. To start the game, Hubbell let the first two AL hitters get to base, Charlie Gehringer on a single and Heinie Manush on a base on balls. The Giants' lefty then proceeded to strike out five of the game's most feared hitters in a row—Ruth, Gehrig, Foxx, Al Simmons, and Joe Cronin.

The record stood for 52 years and was finally tied by another southpaw screwball pitcher—Fernando Valenzuela of the Dodgers, who fanned five in 1986.

Willie Mays, Hank Aaron, and Stan Musial hold the record for most times on an All-Star Game roster with 24. Their total was helped by the fact that there were two All-Star Games in the four years between 1959–62; Aaron played in three of those, and both Mays and Musial were there for all four. Cal Ripken Jr. is next in line with 19 All-Star appearances.

Since the All-Star MVP award was given in 1962 (Leon Wagner of the Angels was the first winner), four players have won the award twice: Mays ('63, '68), Steve Garvey ('74, '78), Gary Carter ('81, '84), and Ripken ('91, 2001).

Stuffing the Ballot Box

At the present time the All-Star teams are selected by a combination of votes by fans, players, coaches, and managers. But back in the '50s the fans voted for the starting eight position players, and the managers picked the rest of the team.

One of several changes in the voting procedure was enacted after the Cincinnati Reds fans stuffed the ballot box and chose seven

The National League's David Wright of the New York Mets steals second past American League second baseman Robinson Cano of the New York Yankees during the fifth inning of the All-Star Game on Tuesday, July 13, 2010, in Anaheim, California. *(AP Photo/Mark J. Terrill)*

members of the Reds as starters for the All-Star Game along with the great Stan Musial of the St. Louis Cardinals. That vote left the young outfielders Willie Mays and Hank Aaron, both in the prime of their careers at the time, to be chosen as substitutes.

Reds players elected by the fans were Johnny Temple (2B), Roy McMillan (SS), Don Hoak (3B), Frank Robinson (LF), Gus Bell (CF), Wally Post (RF), and Ed Bailey (C).

Robinson, of course, is one of the sport's all-time greats, and the others were fine major leaguers, but seven All-Star starters from one team? An investigation revealed that the Cincinnati fans accounted for more than half the ballots submitted that year, including many from the newspaper *The Cincinnati Enquirer* with the names of the Reds already filled in.

Commissioner Ford Frick partially overruled the election and installed Mays of the New York Giants and Aaron of the Milwaukee Braves to replace Bell and Post in the starting outfield. Then he changed the procedure to strip fans of their voting rights. From that point on and for a number of years, the players, managers, and coaches picked the whole team until the vote for starters was returned to the fans.

Since 1969, each team is given an equal number of ballots to pass out at games, and precautions have been taken to avoid the ballot-box stuffing, though there have been some glitches.

All in the Family
Two major leaguers and former All-Stars, Sandy Alomar and Bob Boone, have each had two sons make it to the Midsummer Classic. Catcher Sandy Alomar Jr. and second basemen Roberto Alomar

were both multiple qualifiers, while Aaron Boone made it once and his brother Bret was on the AL roster four times.

While the Boones are the only three-generation All-Stars— grandpa Ray made the AL squad in 1954 and 1956—there have been 10 other father-son All-Star combinations. They are (father listed first):

Felipe Alou and Moises Alou
Gus Bell and Buddy Bell
Bobby Bonds and Barry Bonds
Cecil Fielder and Prince Fielder
Ken Griffey Sr. and Ken Griffey Jr.
Jim Hegan and Mike Hegan
Randy Hundley and Todd Hundley
Vern Law and Vance Law
Gary Matthews Sr. and Gary Matthews Jr.
Steve Swisher and Nick Swisher

The Dazzling Dozen

Twelve current members of the Hall of Fame have won the All-Star Game Most Valuable Player Award since it was first presented in 1962:

Willie Mays, Giants (1962 and 1968)
Juan Marichal, Giants (1965)
Brooks Robinson, Orioles (1966)
Tony Perez, Reds (1967)
Willie McCovey, Giants (1969)
Carl Yastrzemski, Red Sox (1970)
Frank Robinson, Orioles (1971)

Joe Morgan, Reds (1972)
Don Sutton, Dodgers (1977)
Gary Carter, Expos (1981 and 1984)
Cal Ripken Jr., Orioles (1991 and 2001)
Kirby Pickett, Twins (1993)

Just think of the All-Star team you can make from this group: 1B Perez; 2B Morgan; SS Ripken; 3B B. Robinson; DH McCovey; LF Yastrzemski; CF Mays; RF F. Robinson; PH Puckett; C Carter; P Marichal and Sutton.

Quiz!

1. Who is the Braves catcher who was named as the MVP of the 2010 All-Star Game?
2. Who were the starting pitchers in the 2010 game?
3. In recent years the fans have voted for a 34th player to complete the two rosters. Who are the two players who won the 2010 All-Star final vote?
4. Where was the 2010 All-Star Game played?
5. Which speedy Rays outfielder took the MVP award in 2009?
6. Name the only father and son who both won the All-Star Game MVP Award.
7. Which American League ace pitched in the most All-Star Games?
8. Who holds the career record for most All-Star Game at-bats?
9. Who was the only player to have won the All-Star Game MVP and the league MVP in the same year?
10. Who hit the only inside-the-park home run in All-Star Game history?
11. Who is the pitcher who holds the record for most All-Star Game wins?
12. Who hit the only Grand Slam in All-Star Game history?
13. Who holds the record for career saves in All-Star competition?
14. Who was the winner of the 2010 Home Run Derby?
15. Who was the winner of the first Home Run Derby, held in 1986?

Answers

1. Brian McCann
2. NL: Ubaldo Jimenez (Rockies); AL: David Price (Rays)
3. NL: Joey Votto (Reds); AL: Nick Swisher (Yankees)
4. Angels Stadium of Anaheim
5. Carl Crawford
6. Ken Griffey Sr. 1980 and Ken Griffey Jr. 1992
7. Roger Clemens, 9
8. Willie Mays, 75
9. Derek Jeter, 2000
10. Ichiro Suzuki, 2007
11. Lefty Gomez, 3
12. Fred Lynn, 1983
13. Mariano Rivera, 4
14. David Ortiz
15. Dave Parker

Ten

Announcers vs. Coaches and Managers

Did you ever imagine who would win an imaginary game pitting the active managers and coaches against a team of active baseball announcers? Well, you won't have to because we've done it for you.

We have put together (big rosters because these guys are going to need frequent substitutions) for both sides and compared and predicted the winner of a seven-game series. Of course, we're rating every former player when he was in his prime.

Here are our choices and scouting reports for the two teams:

Managers and Coaches
First Base: Marc McGwire (Cardinals), Don Mattingly (Dodgers), Jeff Bagwell (Astros)

    Second Base: Willie Randoph (Brewers), Davey Lopes (Phillies)

    Shortstop: Alan Trammell (Cubs), Larry Bowa (Dodgers), Ozzie Guillen (White Sox)

    Third base: Matt Williams (Diamondbacks), Howard Johnson (Mets), Terry Pendleton (Braves)

Outfield: Harold Baines (White Sox), Dwayne Murphy (Blue Jays), Kirk Gibson (Diamondbacks), Don Baylor (Rockies), George Hendrick (Rays)

Catcher: Joe Torre (Dodgers), Ted Simmons (Padres), Mike Scioscia (Angels), Sandy Alomar Jr. (Indians)

Pitchers: Mel Stottlemyre Jr. (Diamondbacks), Tim Belcher (Indians), Rick Honeycutt (Dodgers), John Wetteland (Mariners), Dave Righetti (Giants), Rick Langford (Blue Jays), Roger McDowell (Braves), Bob McClure (Brewers), Andy Hawkins (Rangers), Steve McCatty (Nationals), Bob Apodaca (Rockies), Bud Black (Padres)

Scout says: Catching, first base, and shortstop are obvious strengths. Solid second base and flychasers Hendrick and Murphy make us strong up the middle. Pitching? The bullpen is good, if not that deep. And the starting pitcher is just okay and could really get plastered by the star-studded announcers lineup.

Announcers

First base: Keith Hernandez (Mets), Mark Grace (Diamondbacks)

Second base: Joe Morgan (HOF, Reds), Frank White (Royals)

Shortstop: Barry Larkin (Major League Baseball Network), Nomar Garciaparra (ESPN)

Third base: Ron Santo (Cubs), Aaron Boone (ESPN)

Outfield: Tony Gwynn (HOF, Padres), Ralph Kiner (HOF, Mets), Tony Oliva (Twins), Paul O'Neill (Yankees), Gary Matthews (Phillies), Ken Singleton (Yankees), Dave Winfield (HOF, ESPN)

Catcher: Tim McCarver (Fox), Ray Fosse (A's), Bob Brenly (Cubs)

Pitchers: Jim Palmer (HOF, Orioles), Dennis Eckersley (HOF, TBS), Orel Hershiser (ESPN), John Smoltz (MLB Network), Fernando Valenzuela (Dodgers), Don Sutton (HOF, Braves), Jim

Former big-league catcher Sandy Alomar Jr., now a coach with the Cleveland Indians, would be an excellent choice to catch a game of baseball coaches versus announcers.
(AP Photo/Mark Duncan)

Kaat (Major League Baseball), Jack Morris (Twins), Bert Blyleven (Twins), Tom Glavine (Braves)

Vying for the final position: Rob Dibble (Nationals), David Wells, Al Leiter, Steve Stone (White Sox), Paul Splittorff (Royals), or Ron Darling (Mets).

Scout says: The starting pitching will rule. But if you can get to the starter early, you have a chance because the bullpen has little behind Smoltz and Dibble if he's activated. Also, we're good around the field but could use some more power at first base. There is a team weakness that can be exploited. Most of these guys talk too much and that can be a distraction.

Pick: Announcers on the strength of that starting pitching.

The Entire-Career-for-One-Team Team
(At least ten years in the majors)
Here are three All-Stars teams of players who were in the majors for at least ten years who played their entire career for one team. The first two are teams of Hall of Famers, a National League team and an American League team. And the third group of All-Stars is made up of many of the players not in the Hall of Fame who were so important to their original team that they stayed for an entire career.

Hall of Fame National League
First base: Stan Musial (Cardinals), Bill Terry (Giants)

Second base: Jackie Robinson (Dodgers), Bill Mazeroski (Pirates)

Third base: Mike Schmidt (Phillies), Pie Traynor (Pirates)

Shortstop: Ernie Banks (Cubs), Travis Jackson (Giants), Peewee Reese (Dodgers)

Outfield: Roberto Clemente (Pirates), Tony Gwynn (Padres), Mel Ott (Giants), Willie Stargell (Pirates), Ross Youngs (Giants)

Catcher: Johnny Bench (Reds), Roy Campanella (Dodgers)
Pitchers: Sandy Koufax (Dodgers), Bob Gibson (Cardinals), Carl Hubbell (Giants), Don Drysdale (Dodgers)

Hall of Fame American League
First base: Lou Gehrig (Yankees)
Second base: Charlie Gehringer (Tigers), Bobby Doerr (Red Sox)
Third base: George Brett (Royals), Brooks Robinson (Orioles)
Shortstop: Luke Appling (White Sox), Cal Ripken Jr. (Orioles), Robin Yount (Brewers), Phil Rizzuto (Yankees)
Outfield: Earle Combs (Yankees), Joe Dimaggio (Yankees), Ted Williams (Red Sox), Mickey Mantle (Yankees), Jim Rice (Red Sox), Al Kaline (Tigers), Kirby Puckett (Twins), Carl Yastrzemski (Red Sox)
Catcher: Bill Dickey (Yankees)
Pitchers: Bob Feller (Indians), Bob Lemon (Indians), Addie Joss (Indians), Walter Johnson (Senators), Whitey Ford (Yankees), Red Faber (White Sox), Ted Lyons (White Sox), Jim Palmer (Orioles)

Art Jorgens, We Salute You
You've probably never heard of Arndt "Art" Jorgens. Few of today's baseball fans have. As a matter of fact, Jorgens was probably not known to many fans during his own time. But Jorgens, a reserve catcher for the New York Yankees, shares a distinction with his more illustrious teammates such as Lou Gehrig, Joe Dimaggio, and Bill Dickey.

They all played their entire careers for the Bronx Bombers, which is a claim not even the great Babe Ruth could make.

Jorgens was in a Yankees uniform from 1929–39 as the backup catcher to Hall of Fame member Bill Dickey. It was one of the great Yankees eras that saw them win the World Series six times.

Though he was active for five Fall Classics, he never made an appearance in any of them. And he holds the record for most games being on a World Series roster (23) without ever getting into a game. He didn't make the postseason roster in 1933.

The most he ever caught during a season was 56 games, which he did in both 1932 and 1934 when Dickey was injured. Jorgens came to the plate just 738 times in 11 years, an average of 67 at-bats a season, and he retired with four home runs and 89 RBIs to his credit.

We have to assume that he was a pretty good defensive catcher and that he could call a good game for a great team like the Yankees to have entrusted him with the backup role for 11 years.

While at bat he was someone who could wait out a walk. His .238 lifetime batting average swells to a .317 OBP (on-base percentage).

So in tribute to his patience and his ability to answer the call when he was needed, we include Art Jorgens on our "Entire Career for One Team, Not in the Hall of Fame" roster. And not much has changed in the more than 70 years since Jorgens last wore the pinstripes. On our team, he's backing up Yankees greats Thurman Munson and Jorge Posada.

One-Team Players Who Are Not in the Hall of Fame

Obviously some of the modern players such as Derek Jeter and Mariano Rivera will be elected to Cooperstown some day. Here is the one-team-for-an-entire-career squad of non–Hall of Famers. This includes active players who have been with only one team for ten years.

First base: Jeff Bagwell (Astros), Albert Pujols (Cardinals), Ken Hrbek (Twins), Todd Helton (Rockies), Joe Collins (Yankees)

Second base: Craig Biggio (Astros), Bobby Richardson (Yankees), Lou Whitaker (Tigers), Jim Gilliam (Dodgers), Gil McDougald (Yankees), Frank White (Royals)

Third base: Al Rosen (Indians), Chipper Jones (Braves), Jim Gantner (Brewers), Stan Hack (Cubs), Pepper Martin (Cardinals), Red Rolfe (Yankees), Ossie Bluege (Senators)

Shortstop: Alan Trammell (Tigers), Derek Jeter (Yankees), Barry Larkin (Reds), Dave Concepcion (Reds), Cecil Travis (Senators), Bill Russell (Dodgers), Frank Crosetti (Yankees)

Outfield: Dom Dimaggio (Red Sox), Bernie Williams (Yankees), Tony Oliva (Twins), Jo Jo Moore (Giants), Bob Allison (Twins), Terry Moore (Cardinals), Roy White (Yankees), Vernon Wells (Blue Jays), Carl Furillo (Dodgers), Mike Greenwell (Red Sox), Tommy Henrich (Yankees), Buddy Lewis (Senators)

Catcher: Thurman Munson (Yankees), Bill Freehan (Tigers), Jorge Posada (Yankees), Wes Westrum (Giants), Harry Danning (Giants), Art Jorgens (Yankees)

Designated Hitter: Edgar Martinez (Mariners)

Pitchers: Ron Guidry (Yankees), J.R. Richard (Astros), Mariano Rivera (Yankees), Dennis Leonard (Royals), Mel Parnell (Red Sox), Steve Rogers (Expos), Ed Rommel (A's), Carl Erskine (Dodgers), Tommy Bridges (Tigers), Paul Splittorff (Royals), Hal Schumacher (Giants), Mel Harder (Indians)

Eleven

Great Baseball Names

In 1962 during a game between the Mets and the Cubs, the Mets'
"Marvelous" Marv Throneberry hit a two-run triple. When he stopped
at third, Cubs first baseman Ernie Banks called for the ball and
appealed to the ump that Throneberry had missed first base.

The appeal was upheld and Throneberry was called out.

The Mets manager Casey Stengel ran out to argue the call until
umpire Dusty Boggess said, "Forget it Casey. He didn't touch second,
either."

Let's say you're writing a novel for the youth market,
or producing a kid's movie about baseball, or crafting a
cartoon or comic strip or book about a baseball hero.
And you're looking for names for your characters.

Look no further than the various baseball encyclopedias and
statistical websites, because through the history of the sport there
have been hundreds of players whose names seem to come right
out of the pages of fiction

Many of these players seemed as if they were destined to
become major league players simply because of their names.

Listed below are three teams of the greatest names in baseball history, the guys who had MLB written in their futures.

Now this is a subjective list, so we realize our inclusion of some of our players was influenced by our knowledge of them as ballplayers. Is Derek Jeter a great baseball name because Derek Jeter has it? We don't think so, but who knows?

It doesn't matter. They're in our baseball names Hall of Fame anyway because their names have taken on a fictional quality

Just remember, we're not poking fun at anyone's name. We're standing here in complete admiration that what their parents named them at birth—or what they came to be called, turned out to be the perfect moniker for their chosen occupation. (Barry Foote probably should have been a podiatrist or Lem Barker a veterinarian.)

Here's our first All-Star name team—with three variations. The players on the first are listed by their real first or middle names or a version of that name (e.g. Ty Cobb is Tyrus Cobb). You couldn't have chosen a better name for a baseball player if you were making it up.

The second team is a list of players who needed their nicknames to rise to the level of fictional hero or villain. And, finally, we have a team of perfectly fine names that are identified by a nickname that was added. Ted Williams is Ted Williams, but he's also called the "Splendid Splinter."

Because these lists are much longer than the others, these teams will definitely have an advantage in depth. So we'll skip the in-depth scouting report.

*Note: I'm sure we're missing some. If you think of any, you're welcome to write them down and make your own list or all-name team. How much time do you think a person can spend on this silliness?

Great Real Names

First basemen: Jimmie Foxx (HOF), Orlando Cepeda (HOF), Ferris Fain, Lu Blue, Dee Fondy, Prince Fielder

Second basemen: Rogers Hornsby, Rod Carew, Napoleon Lajoie

Third basemen: Stan Hack, Ossie Bluege

Shortstops: Nomar Garciaparra, Derek Jeter, Johnny Pesky, Sibby Sisti

Outfielders: Mickey Mantle (HOF), Ty Cobb (HOF), Tris Speaker (HOF), Elmer Flick (HOF), Drungo Hazewood, Willie Mays (HOF), Lastings Milledge, Roberto Clemente (HOF), Mel Ott (HOF), Darryl Strawberry, Rocky Colavito, Vada Pinson, Smead Jolley, Fielder Jones, So Taguchi

Catchers: Earl Battey, Quincy Trouppe, Matt Batts, Wes Westrum, Manny Sanguillen, Pythias Russ, Johnny Kling

Pitchers: Waite Hoyt (HOF), Eppa Rixey (HOF), Van Lingle Mungo, Addie Joss (HOF), Juan Marichal (HOF), Urban Shocker, Vida Blue, Burleigh Grimes (HOF), Orval Overall, Nap Rucker, Terris McDuffie, Mariano Rivera, Early Wynn (HOF), Garland Buckeye, Flint Rhem, Elroy Face, Emil Yde, Virgil Trucks, Jair Jurrjens, Herb Score

Great Nicknames That Replaced Names

And now the all-nickname team. We're not using nicknames that were added to the person's name such as Stan "The Man" Musial. These are nicknames that in the public's mind replaced the player's first name.

Note: We did not list the person's first name because that doesn't help prove our point. We did not include any ethnic references but did include a couple of "Leftys" and "Reds" if it made the player seem like a fictional character.

First basemen: Kitty Bransfield, Boog Powell, Cotton Nash
   Second basemen: Bingo DeMoss, Shooty Babitt
   Third basemen: Pie Traynor (HOF), Home Run Baker (HOF),
Cookie Lavagetto, Red Rolfe, Chipper Jones
   Shortstops: Peewee Reese (HOF), Arky Vaughan (HOF),
Pumpsie Green
   Outfielders: Babe Ruth (HOF), Cool Papa Bell (HOF), Mule
Suttles (HOF), Duke Snider (HOF), Coco Crisp, Gavvy Cravath,
Ducky Medwick (HOF), Suitcase Simpson, Kiki Cuyler (HOF), Goose
Goslin (HOF), Baby Doll Jacobson, Birdie Cree, Braggo Roth, Turkey
Stearnes (HOF), Ping Bodie, Hoot Evers
   Catchers: Yogi Berra (HOF), Biff Pocoroba, Muddy Ruel, Birdie
Tebbetts, Choo-Choo Coleman, Boileryard Clarke
   Pitchers: Satchel Paige (HOF), Dizzy Dean (HOF), Three-Finger
Brown (HOF), Lefty Grove (HOF), Lefty Gomez (HOF), Red Ruffing
(HOF), Schoolboy Rowe, Catfish Hunter (HOF), Blue Moon Odom,
Boof Bonser, Mudcat Grant, Hooks Dauss, Iron Man McGinnity
(HOF), Bo Belinsky, Brickyard Kennedy, Deacon Phillippe, Dizzy
Trout

Nicknames That Add to the Player's Mystique
First basemen: David Ortiz "Big Papi," Frank Thomas "The Big
Hurt," Mike Hargrove "The Human Rain Delay," Fred McGriff
"The Crime Dog," Lou Gehrig "The Iron Horse," Dick Stuart
"Dr. Strangeglove," Frank Chance "The Peerless Leader," Ted
Kluszewski "Big Klu"
   Second basemen: Johnny "The Human Crab" Evers, Kid
Elberfeld "The Tabasco Kid," Bob Ferguson "Death to Flying
Things," Frankie Frisch "The Fordham Flash," Charlie Gehringer
"The Mechanical Man," Tony Lazzeri "Poosh 'Em Up," Pete Rose
"Charlie Hustle"

David "Big Papi" Ortiz has a classic hitter's stance in the batter's box and one of the best nicknames in baseball. *(AP Photo/Ted S. Warren)*

Third basemen: Pablo Sandoval "Kung Fu Panda," Pepper Martin "The Wild Horse of the Osage," Brooks Robinson "Hoover" or "The Vacuum Cleaner," Buck Weaver "The Ginger Kid"

Shortstop: Derek Jeter "Captain Clutch" or "Mr. November," Marty Marion "Mr. Shortstop," "The Octapus," or" Slats," Honus Wagner "The Flying Dutchman," Luke Appling "Old Aches and Pains"

Outfield: Vladimir Guerrero "Vlad the Impaler," Carl Crawford "The Perfect Storm," Shane Victorino "The Flyin' Hawaiian," Carlos Lee "El Caballo," Stan "The Man" Musial, Ted Williams "The Splendid Splinter," Paul Waner "Big Poison," Lloyd Waner "Little Poison," Ty Cobb "The Georgia Peach," Tris Speaker "The Gray Eagle," Babe Ruth "The Bambino" or "The Sultan of Swat," Rusty Staub "La Grande Orange," Lenny "Nails" Dykstra, Hank Aaron "Bad Henry" or "Hammerin' Hank," Willie Mays "The Say Hey Kid," Jason Heyward "The Jay-Hey Kid," Joe Dimaggio "The Yankee Clipper," Earl Averill "The Earl of Snohomish," Mickey Mantle "The Commerce Comet," "Bucketfoot" Al Simmons, Jimmy Wynn "The Toy Cannon," Reggie Jackson "Mr. October," Carl Furillo "The Reading Rifle," Clint Hartung "The Hondo Hurricane"

Catcher: Roger Bresnahan "The Duke of Tralee," Clint Courtney "Scrap Iron"

Pitchers: Mariano Rivera "Sandman," Tim Lincecum "The Freak," Brian Wilson "The Beard," Lon Warneke "The Arkansas Hummingbird," Dick "The Monster" Radatz, Whitey Ford "The Chairman of the Board," Burleigh Grimes "Ol' Stubblebeard," Walter Johnson "The Big Train," Juan Marichal "The Dominican Dandy," Christy Mathewson "Big Six," Herb Pennock "The Knight of Kennett Square," Amos Rusie "The Hoosier Thunderbolt," Al Hrabosky "The Mad Hungarian," Sal "The Barber" Maglie, Sam Leever "The Goshen

Schoolmaster," Vic Raschi "The Springfield Rifle," Ron Guidry "Louisiana Lightnin'"

Manager: Leo "The Lip" Durocher, Connie Mack "The Grand Old Man of Baseball," John McGraw "Little Napoleon," Casey Stengel "The Old Perfessor"

Executive: Branch Rickey "The Mahatma"

Twelve

Big Moments in 2010

April 12: The Minnesota Twins played their first regular season game in Target Field, their new home stadium. It was a 5–2 win over the Red Sox.

April 12: Ivan Rodriguez became the 23rd player to hit 550 career doubles when he hit a two-bagger in the 6th inning against the Phillies.

April 17: Ubaldo Jimenez threw the first no-hitter in the Rockies 18-year history when he shut out the Braves 4–0. It was the first no-hitter of the season.

May 7: Jamie Moyer at 47 years, 170 days became the oldest pitcher in baseball history to throw a complete-game shutout when he defeated the Braves 7–0. Before that, the oldest players to accomplish the feat were Phil Niekro of the Braves and Satchel Paige of the St. Louis Browns, who were both beyond their 46th birthdays at the time. Moyer also became the first pitcher to throw a complete-game shutouts in four different decades (the 1980s, 1990s, 2000s, and 2010s).

May 9: On Mother's Day, Dallas Braden of the A's pitched the 19th perfect game in major league history, a 4–0 win over the Rays. It was the second perfect game in A's history. Jim "Catfish" Hunter threw the first on May 8, 1968, a 4–0 victory over the Twins.

May 23: Trevor Hoffman of the Brewers became the 14th pitcher to appear in 1,000 games when he came in from the bullpen in the 8th inning of a 4–3 win over the Twins.

May 29: Roy Halladay of the Phillies threw the 20th perfect game in major league history when he defeated the Marlins 1–0. It was the first time in the modern baseball era (since 1901) that two perfect games were pitched in the same season. It was the Phillies' first perfect game since Jim Bunning pitched one against the Mets and won 6–0 on Father's Day, June 21, 1964.

May 31: Manny Ramirez hit his 550th career home run against the Diamondbacks, becoming the 14th player to reach that mark.

June 2: Armando Galarraga of the Tigers almost threw the third perfect game of the season in a 3–0 victory over the Indians. However, on what would have been the final out of the game, on a flip to Galarraga from first baseman Miguel Cabrera umpire Jim Joyce mistakenly called the runner safe. Replays clearly showed the runner was out. "I just cost Galarraga a perfect game," Joyce said later. "I thought he beat the throw." Postgame efforts to persuade Major League Baseball to overturn the decision and award Galarraga with a perfect game were unsuccessful.

June 8: Stephen Strasburg of the Nationals became the first pitcher in Major League Baseball history to throw at least 11 strikeouts and issue no walks in his major league debut when he defeated the Pirates 5–2. In the seven innings he worked, he fell one strikeout short of the major league debut record since 1920 held jointly by J.R. Richard of the Astros and Karl Spooner of the Brooklyn Dodgers.

June 18: Strasburg struck out 10 members of the White Sox to set a Major League Baseball record with a total of 32 strikeouts in his first three major league starts, breaking Richard's record. He went on to break the record with a total of 41 strikeouts in his

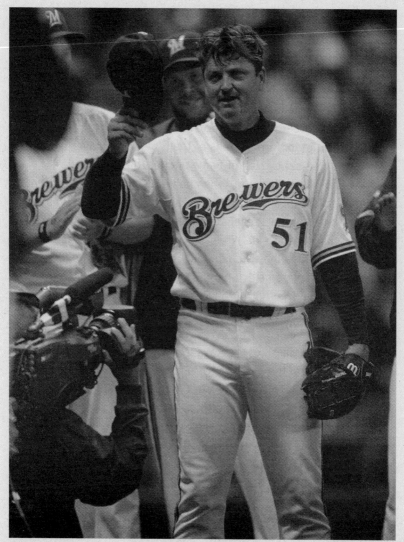

Milwaukee Brewers relief pitcher Trevor Hoffman celebrates after the ninth inning of a game against the St. Louis Cardinals on Tuesday, September 7, 2010, in Milwaukee. Hoffman picked up his career 600th save as the Brewers won 4–2. *(AP Photo/Morry Gash)*

first four big league starts when he struck out nine Royals on **June 23**. Herb Score had set the record with 40 for the 1955 Indians. On **August 27** Strasburg was shut down for the season, and he'll probably miss next year as well because he's undergoing Tommy John surgery to repair his elbow.

June 23: Jamie Moyer broke the record for home runs allowed in a pitcher's career when he surrendered his 506th homer, a third inning home run to Vernon Wells of the Blue Jays. Moyer broke the record that was set by Hall of Fame pitcher Robin Roberts.

June 25: Edwin Jackson, when he was still a member of the Diamondbacks, threw a 1–0 no-hitter against the Rays. It was the fourth no-hitter of the season, counting the two perfect games. Jackson was traded to the White Sox shortly before the trading deadline. The only other Diamondbacks no-hitter was Randy Johnson's perfect game against the Braves in 2004.

June 25: Billy Wagner of the Braves became the fifth reliever in history to record 400 saves when he closed the game over the Tigers.

July 26: Matt Garza of the Rays threw the team's first no-hitter ever when he beat the Tigers 5–0. Garza faced the minimum of 27 batters in the game, giving up a walk in the 2nd inning. Counting the two perfect games, it was the fifth no-hitter of the season.

August 4: Alex Rodriguez of the Yankees became the seventh player in baseball history to reach 600 career home runs when he homered against the Blue Jays. A-Rod, who was 35 years and 8 days old, became the youngest player to reach the mark and was 188 days younger than Babe Ruth when he reached that plateau. Ruth, however, did it in the fewest at-bats with 6,921, followed by Barry Bonds in 8,211 and Sammy Sosa in 8,637.

August 4: When Chipper Jones scored a run in a game against the Mets, he became the 70th player to reach the 1,500 mark in runs scored.

Chipper Jones of the Atlanta Braves connects for a solo home run against New York Mets starter Mike Pelfrey during the third inning on August 4, 2010, at Turner Field in Atlanta.
(AP Photo/Gregory Smith)

August 5: Juan Pierre of the White Sox registered his 500th career stolen base against the Tigers and became the 37th player in major league history to do so.

August 9: David Price of the Rays set a team one-season victory record when he beat the Tigers to record his 15th win. James Shields (2008), Edwin Jackson (2008), and Rolando Arrojo (1998) shared the old Rays record of 14.

August 11: The Yankees' Mariano Rivera became the second reliever to reach 550 career saves when he closed out a victory over the Rangers. Trevor Hoffman is the only man ahead of Rivera on the list.

August 11: Dave Bush of the Brewers became only the third pitcher in baseball history to give up four consecutive home runs when the Diamondbacks' Adam LaRoche, Miguel Montero, Mark Reynolds, and Stephen Drew each put one over the fence in a span of 10 pitches.

August 15: Albert Pujols became the first player in major league history to begin a career with 10 straight 30-plus homer seasons by hitting a home run on August 15.

August 26: Albert Pujols became the 47th player and the third youngest to hit his 400th career home run against the Nationals. Pujols reached the 400 mark at 30 years, 222 days. Alex Rodriguez is the youngest, having done it at 29 years, 316 days, and Ken Griffey Jr. is second at 30 years, 141 days.

September 6: Alex Rodriguez batted in two runs with a home run and a sacrifice fly to go over the 100-RBI mark for the season to become the first man ever to reach that plateau 14 times in a career. In establishing the new record, A-Rod passed Babe Ruth, Lou Gehrig, and Jimmie Foxx.

September 7: Milwaukee Brewers closer Trevor Hoffman, baseball's all-time career saves leader, reached the 600-save mark by finishing the Brewers' 4–3 victory over the St. Louis Cardinals. It was the ninth save in 13 chances this season for Hoffman, who spent most of his career with the San Diego Padres.

September 19: Troy Tulowitzki of the Colorado Rockies joined Albert Belle (1995) and Barry Bonds (2001) as the only major leaguers since 1900 to hit 14 home runs in a span of 15 games, when he homered twice in a win over the Dodgers.

September 19: Bobby Abreu of the Angels homered twice in a victory over the Rays giving him nine seasons with at least 20 homers, 20 stolen bases, and 30 doubles. The only two people with more are Barry Bonds and Bobby Bonds, who did it 10 times.

September 23: Ichiro Suzuki of the Mariners became the first player in history to record at least 200 hits in 10 consecutive seasons, surpassing Ty Cobb who did it in nine consecutive seasons. Pete Rose also has 10 200-hit seasons but not consecutively.

September 25: Rangers closer Neftali Feliz recorded his 38th save of the season against the Athletics, giving him the record for most saves by a rookie in a single season.

October 2: Jose Bautista of the Blue Jays became the seventh player in major league history to produce 50 home runs, 100 walks, and 30 doubles in the same season. Others who accomplished that feat are: Barry Bonds, Jimmie Foxx, Luis Gonzalez, Babe Ruth, Sammy Sosa, and Hack Wilson.

October 6: Roy Halladay of the Phillies pitched the first postseason no-hitter since Don Larsen's perfect game in the 1956 World Series, when he no-hit the Reds in a 4–0 victory in Game 1 of the National League Division Series. Halladay, who had pitched a perfect game earlier in the season, walked Jay Bruce in the fifth inning to come up short of a perfect game. Halladay became the first pitcher to hurl two no-hitters in one season since Nolan Ryan in 1973.

Five players homered in their first major league at-bat. Daniel Nava of the Red Sox on June 12 and J.P. Arencibia on August 7 both did it on the first major league pitch they faced. Jason Heyward of the Braves on April 5, Luke Hughes of the Twins on April 29, and Starlin Castro of the Cubs on May 7 all accomplished this later in the count.

American League Batting Leaders for 2010
Average: Josh Hamilton, Rangers .359
Home Runs: Jose Bautista, Blue Jays 54
RBI: Miguel Cabrera, Tigers 126
Hits: Ichiro Suzuki, Mariners 214
Runs: Mark Teixeira, Yankees 113
Stolen Bases: Juan Pierre, White Sox 68

National League Batting Leaders for 2010
Average: Carlos Gonzalez, Rockies .336
Home Runs: Albert Pujols, Cardinals 42
RBIs: Albert Pujols, Cardinals 118
Hits: Carlos Gonzalez, Rockies 197
Runs: Albert Pujols, Cardinals 115
Stolen bases: Michael Bourne, Astros 52

American League Pitching Leaders for 2010
Wins: CC Sabathia, Yankees 21
ERA: Felix Hernandez, Mariners 2.27
Strikeouts: Jered Weaver, Angels 233
Innings Pitched: Felix Hernandez, Mariners 249. 2
Saves: Rafael Soriano, Rays 45

Quiz!

1. Who is the only player whose number has been retired by all 30 teams?
2. What is that number?
3. When that number was retired in 1997, active players who wore the number were permitted to continue wearing it. There were three players wearing it at the time and only one is still active. Who is he?
4. The Yankees have retired all their single-digit uniform numbers but two: No. 2 and No. 6. But they're expected to retire those numbers in the future. Who are the two Yankees who will be honored when those numbers are retired? One is an active player. The other was a great major league player but not for the Yankees—instead, he was one of the team's most successful managers.
5. One number has been retired by nine teams, the most in baseball. What number is this?
6. The Yankees retired the No. 8 in honor of two great catchers. Can you name them?
7. What player was the first to have his number retired? Name the player and the team, and what was his number? (Hint: It was in 1939.)
8. Nine former players and managers have been honored by having their numbers retired by at least two teams. But only one person has seen his number retired by three teams. Who was this pitcher, and what are the three teams who retired his number?
9. Name the old-time singer and cowboy actor who was the owner of a big league club that retired the No. 26 in his name because his influence and support made him the team's 26th man on the roster.
10. The only No. 22 ever retired was to honor this American League pitcher, who was an eight-time 20-game winner.

National League Pitching Leaders for 2010
Wins: Roy Halladay, Phillies 21
ERA: Josh Johnson, Marlins 2:30
Strikeouts: Tim Lincecum, Giants 231
Innings Pitched: Roy Halladay, Phillies 250.2
Saves: Brian Wilson, Giants 48

2010 AL Playoff Teams
Eastern Division Champions: Tampa Bay Rays
Central Division Champions: Minnesota Twins
Western Division Champions: Texas Rangers
Wild Card: New York Yankees

Division Series
Rangers defeated the Rays 3–2
Yankees defeated the Twins 3–0

League Champion Series
Rangers defeated the Yankees 4–2

American League Champions
Texas Rangers

2010 NL Playoff Teams
Eastern Division Champions: Philadelphia Phillies
Central Division Champions: Cincinnati Reds
Western Division Champions: San Francisco Giants
Wild Card: Atlanta Braves

Division Series
Phillies defeated the Reds 3–0
Giants defeated the Braves 3–1

League Championship Series
Giants defeated the Phillies 4–2

National League Champions
San Francisco Giants

World Series
Giants defeated the Rangers 4–1

Retired Numbers
Five teams retired numbers during the 2010 season.

June 26: The Giants retired the No. 20 worn by Monte Irvin, one of the first African Americans to play in the major leagues for the New York Giants. Irvin, who starred in the Negro Leagues as a young man, is a member of the Baseball Hall of Fame.

July 3: The Cardinals retired the No. 24 worn by former manager Whitey Herzog, who entered the Hall of Fame later in the month.

August 6: Prior to the 20,000th game in franchise history, the Braves retired the No. 47 worn by Tom Glavine.

August 7: The Diamondbacks retired the No. 20 worn by Luis Gonzalez, one of the team's most popular players. "Gonzo" hit the walk-off single in the seventh game of the 2001 World Series off Mariano Rivera to clinch the team's first and only World Championship.

August 29: The White Sox retired the No. 35 worn by their great first baseman Frank Thomas before their game against the New York Yankees.

Soon the Yankees May Have To Go To Three-Digit Numbers

In addition to Jackie Robinson, who only played for the Brooklyn Dodgers, the Yankees have retired 15 uniform numbers honoring 16 players and managers, the most in baseball:

No. 1 Billy Martin, 2b, mgr.

No. 3 Babe Ruth, rf

No. 4 Lou Gehrig, lb

No. 5 Joe Dimaggio, cf.

No. 7 Mickey Mantle, cf

No. 8 Bill Dickey, c, Yogi Berra, c, mgr

No. 9 Roger Maris, rf

No. 10 Phil Rizzuto, ss

No. 15 Thurman Munson, c

No. 16 Whitey Ford, p

No. 23 Don Mattingly, lb

No. 32 Elston Howard, c

No. 37 Casey Stengel, mgr.

No. 44 Reggie Jackson, of

No. 49 Ron Guidry, p

Thirteen

The Match Game

I. Match the Major League Player With the Country of His Birth

1. Alex Rodriguez

2. Joey Votto

3. Edgar Renteria

4. Alex Rios

5. Albert Pujols

6. Johan Santana

7. Andrew Jones

8. Carlos Lee

9. Kendry Morales

10. Joakim Soria

A. Venezuela

B. Puerto Rico

C. U.S.

D. Curacao

E. Mexico

F. Cuba

G. Panama

H. Dominican Republic

I. Canada

J. Columbia

Answers: 1-C, 2-I, 3-J, 4-B, 5-H, 6-A, 7-D, 8-G, 9-F, 10-E

II. Match the Team with the Ballpark It Currently Calls Home

1. New York Mets

2. Florida Marlins

3. Detroit Tigers

4. Boston Red Sox

5. Minnesota Twins

6. San Diego Padres

7. Chicago White Sox

8. Philadelphia Phillies

9. Seattle Mariners

10. Houston Astros

A. U.S. Cellular Field

B. Citi Field

C. Target Center

D. Safeco Field

E. Land Shark Stadium

F. Petco Park

G. Comerica Park

H. Citizens Bank Park

I. Fenway Park

J. Minute Maid Park

Answers: 1-B, 2-E, 3-G, 4-I, 5-C, 6-F, 7-A, 8-H, 9-D 10-J

III. Match the Team with the Old Ballpark It Used To Call Home

1. New York Giants	A. Briggs Stadium
2. Washington Senators	B. Ebbets Field
3. Pittsburgh Pirates	C. Shea Stadium
4. Cincinnati Reds	D. The Astrodome
5. Philadelphia Phillies	E. Forbes Field
6. Brooklyn Dodgers	F. Crosley Field
7. Detroit Tigers	G. Griffith Stadium
8. Chicago White Sox	H. Connie Mack Stadium
9. New York Mets	I. The Polo Grounds
10. Houston Astros	J. Comiskey Park

Answers: 1-I, 2-G, 3-E, 4-F, 5-H, 6-B, 7-A, 8-J, 9-C, 10-D

IV. Match the Historic Team from the Past and the Nickname It Is Remembered By (They were not all World Championship teams.)

1. The Big Red Machine

2. The Hitless Wonders

3. The Idiots

4. The Mustache Gang

5. Murderers' Row

6. We Are Family

7. The Gas House Gang

8. The Boys of Summer

9. Harvey's Wallbangers

10. The Southside Hitmen

A. Pittsburgh Pirates 1979

B. Brooklyn Dodgers, early '50s

C. Milwaukee Brewers, early '80s

D. Cincinnati Reds, 1970s

E. St. Louis Cardinals, mid-1930s

F. Chicago White Sox, 1977

G. New York Yankees, 1927

H. Boston Red Sox, 2004

I. Oakland A's, early '70s

J. Chicago White Sox, 1906

Answers: 1-D, 2-J, 3-H, 4-I, 5-G, 6-A, 7-E, 8-B, 9-C, 10-F

V. Match the Hall of Famer with the First Name of His Brother Who Also Played in the Major Leagues.

1. Phil Niekro

2. Joe Dimaggio

3. Hank Aaron

4. Cal Ripken Jr.

5. Dizzy Dean

6. Rick Ferrell

7. Tony Gwynn

8. Gaylord Perry

9. George Brett

10. Joe Sewell

A. Wes

B. Billy

C. Paul

D. Luke

E. Jim

F. Ken

G. Dom

H. Chris

I. Tommie

J. Joe

Answers: 1-J, 2-G, 3-I, 4-B, 5-C, 6-A, 7-H, 8-E, 9-F, 10-H

VI. Match the First Name of the Major League Brothers with the Family Name

1. Felipe, Matty, and Jesus

2. Bengie, Yadier, and Jose

3. Aaron and Bret

4. Sandy Jr. and Roberto

5. Jeff and Jered

6. Jerry Jr. and Scott

7. Adam and Andy

8. Jason and Jeremy

9. Greg and Mike

10. Ramon and Pedro

A. Maddux

B. Alomar

C. Weaver

D. LaRoche

E. Boone

F. Giambi

G. Alou

H. Martinez

I. Molina

J. Hairston

Answers: 1-G, 2-I, 3-E, 4-B, 5-C, 6-J, 7-D, 8-F, 9-A, 10-H

A reporter asked Yogi Berra about his two hits from the previous night when Berra corrected him and said he had three hits.

The reporter apologized. "I checked the paper, and the box score said you had two hits. It must have been a typographical error."

"Hell, no," Yogi said. "It was a clean single to left."

Fourteen

Perfect Pitch

On August 23, 2010, Rays closer Rafael Soriano of the Rays threw an immaculate inning. That means he struck out three batters on nine pitches when he fanned Erick Aybar, Mike Napoli, and Peter Bourjos of the Angels to end the game and gain a 4–3 win for the Rays.

He was only the third pitcher in history to get a save with an immaculate inning. "I didn't know that," Soriano told the *St. Petersburg Times*. "I didn't know until you told me that it was a big deal." It was Soriano's 38th save of the season, and all three batters went down on swinging third strikes.

"Unbelievable, I was kind of giddy out there," said teammate Dan Wheeler, who was in the bullpen watching the ninth inning. "That was impressive, really impressive."

The only pitchers in history who have thrown two immaculate innings are Lefty Grove, Sandy Koufax, and Nolan Ryan. Grove did it twice in the 1928 season.

Nine of the pitchers who have accomplished the feat are Hall of Famers John Clarkson, Rube Waddell, Dazzy Vance, Grove, Jim Bunning, Koufax, Ryan, Bob Gibson, and Bruce Sutter.

The last immaculate inning was thrown by Ross Ohlendorf of the Pirates in the seventh inning of a 2–1 loss to the Cardinals on September 5, 2009.

The following pitchers have also accomplished this feat in the past decade:

Randy Johnson, Arizona Diamondbacks, 2001

Jason Isringhausen, St. Louis Cardinals, 2002

Pedro Martinez, Boston Red Sox, 2002

Brian Lawrence, San Diego Padres, 2002

Brandon Backe, Houston Astros, 2004

LaTroy Hawkins, Chicago Cubs, 2004

Rick Helling, Milwaukee Brewers, 2006

Buddy Carlyle, Atlanta Braves, 2007

Rich Harden, Oakland Athletics, 2008

Felix Hernandez, Seattle Mariners, 2008

A.J. Burnett, New York Yankees, 2009

The last time a major league team had four 20-game winners was the Baltimore Orioles of 1971. Dave McNally won 21 games while Pat Dobson, Mike Cuellar, and Jim Palmer all won 20. All four had ERAs less than 3.10.

The O's won the American League East by 12 games then swept the A's in three games in the AL Championship Series but lost to the Pirates in seven games in the World Series.

In 1959 Lew Burdette was the winning pitcher in one of the most storied games of all time. The Pirates left-hander Harvey Haddix pitched a perfect game against the Braves for 12 innings but lost when Joe Adcock of the Braves hit a home run in the 13th. Burdette, who also went the distance, earned the win.

Seen here recording his 32nd save of the season in a win over the Detroit Tigers on August 9, 2010, Rafael Soriano of the Rays pitched an immaculate inning against the Angels on August 23. *(AP Photo/Duane Burleson)*

When he was negotiating his 1960 contact, Burdette joked with the press that he was the greatest pitcher who ever lived. "The greatest game that was ever pitched in baseball wasn't good enough to beat me, so I've got to be the greatest," he said.

Only eight men in history have been the winning pitcher in the All-Star Game and the World Series in the same season. The last to accomplish this was Josh Beckett of the Boston Red Sox in 2007.

Hoyt Wilhelm was a Hall of Fame pitcher who was famous for throwing an effective knuckleball that kept him in the majors for 21 years. He was the first pitcher to appear in 1,000 games.

In his first at-bat in the majors for the Giants in the Polo Grounds, Wilhelm lifted a home run that fell just over the right-field fence. This was going to be great—the team had a new relief pitcher who was also a hitter. However, in 21 seasons, Wilhelm never hit another homer.

In June 1938, Reds pitcher Johnny Vander Meer set a record that many experts believe will never be duplicated. He threw two no-hitters on back-to-back starts.

On June 11, he no-hit the Braves and then beat the Dodgers 6–0 on June 15 in the first night game at Ebbets Field in Brooklyn. The feat earned him the permanent nickname of Johnny "Double No-Hit" Vander Meer.

The New York Mets, the San Diego Padres, and the Tampa Bay Rays are the only teams whose pitchers have never pitched a no-hitter. The Dodgers lead baseball in most no-hitters in history with 20. The Phillies and the Braves lead in most no-hitters pitched against them with 17 each. In 1990 the American League had six no-hit games, which is the most either league has ever had in one season.

How can a pitcher record six consecutive strikeouts in one half-inning? Though it's not likely to occur, here's how it could happen.

1. The first two batters strike out.
2. The third batter strikes out but the catcher drops the ball and the runner reaches first.
3. The runner steals second.
4. The fourth batter strikes out and the catcher commits another error, so the runner reaches first. Now there are runners on first and second with two out.
5. The runners then execute the perfect double-steal. Runners on second and third with two out.
6. The fifth batter strikes out and the catcher, who's really begging to be sent to the minors, drops the third strike for the third time. The runner reaches first and now the bases are loaded with two out.
7. The sixth batter strikes out, ending the inning. The pitcher gets credit for six strikeouts, but he's not talking to his catcher any more.

Fifteen

Baseball Odds and Ends

Mattingly's Managing Gaffe

The Giants beat the Dodgers 7–5 in a July game in 2010 thanks in part to an umpire's decision about the rule governing a manager's trip to the mound to talk to his pitcher—or anyone else for that matter.

With the Dodgers leading 5–4 in the top of the ninth and manager Joe Torre ejected earlier because of an exchange of beanballs, acting manager Don Mattingly brought in closer Jonathan Broxton to finish the Giants off. However, Broxton gave up a single, a walk, and an intentional walk to load the bases with one out.

Out came Mattingly to talk things over with his pitcher. After finishing the discussion, Mattingly took a step or two off the mound when first baseman James Loney asked the acting skipper a question.

Mattingly stepped back on the corner of the mound to answer the question and then headed back to the dugout.

Giants' manager Bruce Bochy then came out on the field and argued that Mattingly's stepping back on the mound constituted a second trip to the mound and that, according to the rules, the pitcher had to be removed.

The umpires deliberated and agreed with Bochy. They ordered Broxton removed and replaced immediately and that the new pitcher didn't have the right to warm up.

George Sherrill came in after only three tosses in the bullpen and, on his second pitch, gave up a two-run double to Andres Torres, giving the Giants the lead. The Giants added an insurance run and retired the Dodgers in the bottom of the ninth for the win.

Bochy was correct in his assertion that Mattingly's leaving the dirt circle of the mound completed his first visit and when he stepped back on it was technically a second trip to the mound. That meant Broxton was gone and with him quite possibly the ball game.

The Long, Slow Walk

When the Red Sox lost 7–2 to the Angels on August 19, 2010, Boston avoided a 10–0 sweep of the season series against the team that swept them out of last year's ALDS, 3–0.

It brought to mind the champion 1969 Miracle Mets, a team that went 100–62 in the regular season (107–63 counting the postseason) but suffered 10 of those losses to a Houston team that finished 81–81.

The Mets took 2-of-3 from the Astros the first time the teams met. They were then outscored by Houston 66–21 in losing nine games in a row.

Particularly memorable was a doubleheader on July 30 at New York's Shea Stadium in which Houston scored 27 runs. The Astros scored 11 runs in the ninth inning of the first game, but then when they were in the middle of a 10-run third inning in Game 2,

Mets Manager Gil Hodges made a rare move that was intended to humiliate a ballplayer he felt wasn't hustling.

Mets leftfielder Cleon Jones, the team's best hitter, was a little lackadaisical on several balls hit his way. That's when Hodges removed him from the game. But the way he did it sent a message to Jones and the entire team. Hodges didn't signal his outfielder in from the dugout or relay the message through a coach to tell Jones to come out.

No, Hodges walked slowly and deliberately all the way to left field and escorted Jones back to the dugout. Jones never dogged it again and, after a loss to the Astros the next day, the Mets went 45–18 the rest of the season to overtake the league-leading Cubs for the pennant. The New Yorkers then went 7–1 in the postseason (there were only two rounds of playoffs then) to win the World Championship.

Babe Ruth's Running Blunder Loses Series

Question: Who was the only player in the history of baseball who was "caught stealing" with two outs in the ninth inning of the seventh game of the World Series?

Answer: Babe Ruth.

That's the truth. Ruth had just had one of the best years of his career, .372 batting average, 47 HR, and 146 RBIs. In Game 4 of the Series, he had hit three home runs. Then in Game 7 Ruth came to the plate with two out in the bottom of the ninth and the Yankees trailing 3–2.

The great Pete Alexander, who was in the twilight of his career, was on in relief for the Cardinals and one out away from victory. He walked the Babe.

With Bob Meusel at bat and Lou Gehrig on deck, Ruth shocked everyone by taking off for second base. Catcher Bob O'Farrell gunned it to Rogers Hornsby at second in plenty of time to tag Ruth, and the Cardinals wrapped up their first world championship.

Babe said he did it because he thought no one would expect him to steal, but the Cardinals seemed ready.

To this day, that's the only World Series that ended with a "caught stealing."

Sausage Shenanigans

On July 9, 2003, in Milwaukee, between innings of a game between the visiting Pittsburgh Pirates and the host Brewers, an incident occurred that will forever be known as "Wienergate."

In a popular promotional race that involved young people dressed up as sausage mascots representing the various products of the Klement Sausage Company, there was an interference call that led to the arrest of a member of the Pirates.

As the racing sausages passed the Pittsburgh dugout, first baseman Randall Simon swung a bat at the Italian Sausage's head. Though the bat didn't hit her head, the woman inside the costume fell over and knocked down the Hot Dog, as well. The Polish Sausage came to the rescue and helped the Italian Sausage to her feet, and everyone finished the race.

Simon, who was arrested and paid a fine, later apologized for the incident and said it was an accident.

The woman inside the costume, Mandy Block, asked Simon to autograph the offending bat and give it to her, which he did—ending the sausage saga on an upbeat note.

Nature 3, Baseball 0

The Twins' new ballpark, Target Field, has been visited by a pair of creatures from the animal kingdom in its inaugural year. First it was Kirby the Kestrel, named after the Twins late, great centerfielder Kirby Puckett. This bird, the smallest member of the falcon family, appeared on the right field foul pole and proceeded to swoop down, catch, and devour small insects, including a large moth, to the great amusement of the cheering fans.

This action has been caught on videotape and rerun in slow motion complete with play-by-play commentary from the Minnesota announcers. The bird made at least one other appearance later in the season.

Another entry in the Twins' "zoo parade" arrived on May 25 when a squirrel ran out on the field and interrupted play in the fourth inning of a Yankees-Twins game. The visitor charged at Twins third baseman Brendan Harris and then ran to the outfield wall to try to escape. It remained on the field as play resumed and then ran the length of the outfield warning track to find a way out with the crowd chanting, "Let's go squirrel."

What happened in San Diego in July caused even more of a buzz. With the Astros leading the Padres 6–1 in the ninth inning of an afternoon game, Padres left fielder Kyle Blanks began moving toward the infield to try to get a timeout called.

An umpire went out to see what the problem was and saw it was a swarm of bees. The players were soon pulled off the field, and several sections of the stands were evacuated.

A masked beekeeper went out and sprayed cans of poison on the bees, picked up the dead intruders, and the crisis was over. The beekeeper left the stadium to the cheers of the excited San Diego fans and even waved back to acknowledge their ovation.

"Bizarre things," Houston's Geoff Blum told the Associated Press. "You think you've seen it all in baseball, and you're going to see something new." After a 52-minute delay, the Astros went on to win 7–2 with Blum getting the big hit, a three-run homer.

Famous Home Run Calls

When you hear the announcer's home run call, "You can put it on the board. Yesssssssss!," you know its Hawk Harrelson speaking, and you also know that a member of the White Sox just "went yard."

Here are some other signature home run calls made famous by popular announcers:

Vin Scully: "Forget It."

Russ Hodges: "Bye bye baby!"

Mel Allen: "Going, going, gone!"

Lon Simmons: "Tell it Good-bye!"

Ernie Harwell: "Long gone!"

Harry Caray: "It could be. It might be. It is. A home run!"

Bob Prince: "Kiss it good-bye!" or "See Ya!"

Chris Berman: "Back, back, back, back"

Bob Uecker: "Get up, get outa here, gone for a home run!"

Harry Kalas: "Watch that baby, outa here!"

Jack Brickhouse: "Hey, hey!"

Ten Baseball Movies You Should See

1. *Pride of the Yankees* (1941): The tragic story of the great Yankees first-baseman Lou Gehrig.
2. *Eight Men Out* (1988): A dramatic historical look at the 1919 World Series and how the White Sox conspired with gamblers and purposely lost the Series.

3. *The Natural* (1984): The movie version of Bernard Malamud's great novel, it's a sports fantasy about a player who comes out of nowhere to become a superstar and miraculously leads a struggling team to the top.

4. *A League of Their Own* (1992): A comedy depicting life in the Women's Professional Baseball League during World War II.

5. *Major League* (1989): A comedy about a woman who buys the Cleveland Indians and does everything to see that they'll lose so she can move the team. The colorful group of has-beens and never-were players find out about her plans and do everything they can to win.

6. *The Bad News Bears* (1976): A comedy about a losing Little League team and its new manager, a down-on-his-luck former coach, who tries to lead them out of the doldrums in a super-competitive league.

7. *The Rookie* (2002): The story of a chemistry professor/baseball coach who tries to rally his troops by promising to go for a big league tryout if they win the championship. When they do, he does, and he discovers his old baseball pitching magic and makes it to the majors.

8. *The Jackie Robinson Story* (1950): A biographical account of Robinson breaking the color barrier in the major leagues in the 1940s in what has become known as "The Great Experiment." Jackie Robinson stars as Jackie Robinson.

9. **61,* (2001): A TV movie examining the 1961 Yankees and good friends Roger Maris and Mickey Mantle as they battle to break Babe Ruth's single-season record of 60 home runs.

10. *Field of Dreams* (1989): A fantasy about an Iowa farmer who hears voices that tell him to build a baseball diamond in his cornfield in order to reconnect with his deceased father and ball players from the past.

Ten Baseball Books You Should Read

1. *Eight Men Out,* Eliot Asinof, (Holt Rinehard Winston, 1963): The story of the many interesting facets of the Black Sox scandal in which the Chicago White Sox purposely lost the 1919 World Series.

2. *Ball Four,* Jim Bouton, (Stein and Day, 1970): A diary of the pitcher's 1969 season and his observations about the game and its personalities. It was very controversial at the time because it showed baseball players as human beings and exposed long-standing myths about the game.

3. *The Long Season*, Jim Brosnan, (Harper and Row, 1960): The first book that caused a stir in baseball as the pitcher frankly wrote about his experiences during the 1959 season.

4. *Only the Ball Was White*, Robert Peterson, (Prentice Hall, 1970): A thorough and early history of the Negro Leagues, the only professional option for black players before Jackie Robinson integrated the major leagues in 1947.

5. *The New Bill James Historical Abstract*, (The Free Press, a division of Simon & Schuster, 2001): A thorough and literate history of baseball, including an evaluation of all the great ballplayers and teams with new statistical formulas to evaluate performance.

6. *The Glory of Their Times*, Lawrence S. Ritter, (MacMillan, 1966): Interviews with old-time ballplayers and their memories of the game in the early decades of the twentieth century.

7. *Nine Innings,* Dan Okrent, (Ticknor and Fields, 1985): An account of major league history, zeroing in on specific subjects for each decade of the twentieth century.

8. *The Boys of Summer*, Roger Kahn, (Harper & Row, 1972): The story of the Brooklyn Dodgers of the 1950s told via interviews with the players long after they retired.

9. *The Era, 1947-57*, Roger Kahn, (Harper & Row, 1993): An examination of New York major league baseball from the year Jackie Robinson broke the color line to the year the Dodgers and Giants moved to the West Coast. It was a period where everything that happened in baseball seemed to happen in New York, including: the major league debut and the struggles of Robinson; the rivalries among the three New York teams; Bobby Thomson's "Shot Heard 'Round the World;" Willie Mays' catch in the 1954 World Series; and Don Larsen's perfect game in the 1956 World Series.

10. *Dynasty: The New York Yankees 1949-1964*, by Peter Golenbeck, (Prentice Hall, 1977): The story of the most incredible run of winning baseball in the history of the game during which the Yankees won the World Series nine times with a cast that over the years included such greats as Joe Dimaggio, Yogi Berra, Whitey Ford, Mickey Mantle, and Roger Maris.

Baseball Poetry
"Spahn and Sain"
By Gerald V. Hern

First we'll use Spahn
Then we'll use Sain
Then an off day
Followed by rain
Back will come Spahn
Followed by Sain
And followed
We hope
By two days of rain

The poem was written in 1948, the year the Boston Braves won the pennant with the pair of pitching aces Warren Spahn and Johnny Sain. Though Spahn is in the Hall of Fame and is considered one of the best southpaws in history, that year Sain, a four-time 20-game winner, was the ace with a 24-15 record. He also led the league in games pitched, games started, complete games, and innings pitched.

"Baseball's Sad Lexicon"
By Franklin Pierce Adams

These are the saddest of possible words:
"Tinker to Evers to Chance."
Trio of bear cubs and fleeter than birds,
Tinker and Evers and Chance
Ruthlessly pricking our gonfalon bubbly
Making a Giant hit into a double-
Words that are heavy with nothing but trouble:
"Tinker to Evers to Chance"

Adams wrote the poem about the famous Cubs double play combination for his column, "Always in Good Humor," in the *Evening Mail* in July 1910 when he was on his way to see the Cubs and Giants play at The Polo Grounds. The original title of the poem was "That Double Play Again?"

Tinker (the shortstop), Evers (the second baseman), and Chance (the first baseman) were key figures in the great Cubs team of the first decade of the 20th century. They won the World Series in both 1907 and 1908. All three players were elected to the Hall of Fame in 1946, and there has always been speculation that the popularity of the poem contributed to their election.

"Take Me Out to the Ball Game"
1908 version
Author: Jack Norworth
Composer: Albert Von Tilzer

Katie Casey was baseball mad.
Had the fever and had it bad;
Just to root for the home town crew,
Ev'ry sou
Katie blew.
On a Saturday, her young beau
Called to see if she'd like to go,
To see a show, but Miss Kate said, "No,
I'll tell you what you can do."

Chorus

"Take me out to the ball game,
Take me out with the crowd
Buy me some peanuts and crackerjack,
I don't care if I never get back,
Let me root, root, root for the home team,
If they don't win it's a shame
For its one, two, three strikes, you're out,
At the old ball game."
Katie Casey saw all the games,
Knew the players by their first names;
Told the umpire he was wrong,
All along, good and strong.
When the score was just two to two
Katie Casey knew what do do,
Just to cheer up the boys she knew,
'She made the gang sing this song.

Repeat Chorus